TRAVELING DIRECTIONS
for WOMEN

ON A JOURNEY OF RECOVERY,
SELF-HEALING AND SELF-DISCOVERY

SHARON M. CADIZ, Ed.D.

BALBOA.
PRESS
A DIVISION OF HAY HOUSE

Balboa Press books may be ordered through booksellers or by contacting:

Balboa Press
A Division of Hay House
1663 Liberty Drive
Bloomington, IN 47403
www.balboapress.com
1-(877) 407-4847

Because of the dynamic nature of the Internet, any web addresses or links contained in this book may have changed since publication and may no longer be valid. The views expressed in this work are solely those of the author and do not necessarily reflect the views of the publisher, and the publisher hereby disclaims any responsibility for them.

The author of this book does not dispense medical advice or prescribe the use of any technique as a form of treatment for physical, emotional, or medical problems without the advice of a physician, either directly or indirectly. The intent of the author is only to offer information of a general nature to help you in your quest for emotional and spiritual well-being. In the event you use any of the information in this book for yourself, which is your constitutional right, the author and the publisher assume no responsibility for your actions.

Any people depicted in stock imagery provided by Thinkstock are models, and such images are being used for illustrative purposes only. Certain stock imagery © Thinkstock.

ISBN: 978-1-4525-7094-5 (sc)
ISBN: 978-1-4525-7095-2 (hc)
ISBN: 978-1-4525-7093-8 (e)

Library of Congress Control Number: 2013905066

Printed in the United States of America.

Balboa Press rev. date: 04/05/2013

INTRODUCTION

"You will be a failure, until you impress the subconscious
with the conviction you are a success. This is done
by making an affirmation which clicks."
Florence Scovel Shinn

Everyday countless women walk into treatment programs, doctor's offices, emergency rooms, therapy sessions and hospitals only to stumble over the remnants of male dominated treatment models, sterile treatment approaches and cold, clinical practices. Once inside they often find themselves struggling in a breathless hurried quest driven by linear, logical external controls that standardize and measure healing by the clock or calendar. Although some succeed in gaining health and healing, many others face incomplete healing, relapse or diminished self-esteem and feelings of failure.

There is common agreement that treatment or healing, like life, is a journey. Travelers on the journey differ, as do the directions they need to follow. When the traveler is a woman, she might need something different from what conventional treatment offers; different traveling directions, if you will.

Women need this handbook because, as stated in the first chapter, "It should not be assumed that change will be a pleasing experience, even if it summons positive change." Realizing that one wants to change is only the first step, and it's the guidance that one follows that is critical to success. The successes of the clients and friends with whom I have shared this book convince me that practitioners and other individuals will find it a valuable resource and travel guide for the journey of a lifetime.

PREFACE

As a woman, clinical practitioner, educator, and former administrator for a women's treatment facility, I speak from a varied experience and perspective on the healing process. Because of my commitment to the women I serve, I have written this handbook entitled, <u>Traveling Directions for Women on a Journey of Recovery, Self-Healing and Self-Discovery.</u> It is intended as a companion to other forms of healing help that are available to support women "through the perilous depths on that inner pathway to healing." In the book, I highlight six (6) areas to explore and a variety of exercises, essays and poems that act as guideposts, roadside tips and "rules" of the road that can direct one along the way. I have offered a variety of creative ways to stay on the path and handle setbacks. In addition, I encourage you to create your own affirmations that anchor your intentions; elevating your self-talk to a higher, positive plane for realization.

When I first began conducting treatment groups for women suffering from chemical dependence, abuse, mental illness and interpersonal trauma, I found myself heavily relying upon what I knew as a woman, mother and educator because the women were multi-dimensional, with many relationships, roles and a need to educate themselves about how to cope with their emotions. What I learned from them about what works in their recovery and healing has been placed in my handbook. Furthermore, I found that what is helpful to these women is, also, beneficial to all women who, over a lifetime, require healing from numerous hurts and life cycle events. Recovery is a mainstream concern whether the challenge is to quit smoking, survive an abusive childhood or thrive following a painful loss or consuming addiction. The absence of self awareness and sustainable methods to approach the challenging changes it requires, can result in aborted lives and diminished opportunities for a bright and hopeful future.

Remember to use this book as a guide; directions for your journey to healing and wholeness. Each early chapter is a guidepost with exercises, quotations, symbols, materials or poems. You are encouraged to add or write your own poetry, select other quotations, symbols or materials. The later chapters give you further guidance and are intended to prompt you to go deeper into your self exploration through the use of testimony and the sharing of life sustaining truths.

The chapters are intended to proceed in sequence; however, like any traveler, you may experience difficulty staying on course, have the need to change direction or rest from time to time. This is no problem because it is presumed that every journey will be different; experienced in unique and special ways by every traveler. This handbook should meet your needs, so when you need to change direction, or course, do so.

You can work through the exercises in groups or on your own. Feel free to pick it up and put it down according to your needs. If you are experiencing a particular crisis, you may want to pick it up, or find that you must stop temporarily either to process a difficult challenge or give yourself time to rest. You can consider photocopying some pages to facilitate re-use. Your responses will likely change over time.

Always endeavor to bring peace into your sessions. Think about opening each session by taking three (3) deep breaths and closing in the same way. You can say an affirmation and/or an inspirational quotation. Try to create a calming serenity for yourself by selecting a suitable environment free of interruptions. You might want to select some tranquil music to enhance your sessions. Making a regular time to do the exercises and read the material is evidence of your commitment to greater self awareness in the direction of meaningful change. It will also start the process of helping you to take up more space in your important life; demonstrating that you matter enough to be scheduled into your busy day. As you move through the handbook you will experience a deeper sense of your personal power. You will be able to safely examine patterns in your life and challenge yourself to move beyond perceived limits to a more intentional, self determined future destination that harmonizes with nature, mind, body and spirit.

It is my sincere hope that this book will offer the kind of help you may need Finally, perhaps we will one day meet on the path and exchange stories about our travels.

Peace be the journey...
Sharon M. Cadiz, Ed.D.

PROLOGUE

GETTING ON THE ROAD

*D*riving to treatment [healing]...

Let's imagine that you are driving to treatment [healing], and you are in your car just driving. It seems like you drive on and on without stopping; suddenly you see a sign that says: "This way to treatment." You think, "Now I'm getting somewhere," and you continue. Again, you drive on and on, and just then a homeless man almost walks into your car; you swerve to miss him and the excitement leaves you shaken. Nonetheless, you keep going.

Weary and somewhat disheartened, you drive on and without warning your front left tire goes flat. You get out and fix it, then get back in the car. Just when you are about to give up, you see another sign that says, "This way to treatment [healing]."

The road winds through seemingly endless curves and suddenly you drive right into a storm. You can't see clearly in front of you because of the sheet of rain pouring onto your car, but you keep going. As fear mounts in your chest and your hands grip the steering wheel in desperation, the sun appears through an opening in the clouds. You start up a hill only to get stuck in some mud that formed during the storm. Thanks to a shovel that you packed, you are able to free your car from the muck and move on.

By the time you reach the top of the hill, you have little hope that you will ever reach your destination, then you see a woman standing on the side of the road and you ask directions, "How do I get to treatment [healing]?" You go on to tell her of your exhausting journey.

The stranger calmly replies, "You've been on the right road all along and the fact that you've gotten this far means your treatment [healing] started when you began on the road long ago." She goes on to say, "Reading the road signs was part of the treatment; swerving to miss hitting that homeless man was part of the treatment, as well as fixing your flat tire and driving through a terrible storm…"

Be aware that on the road to healing, if you are not careful, you could miss it.

6 GUIDEPOSTS ON THE WELLNESS PATH

1. <u>Beginning</u>
[ ] recognizing the desire to heal
[ ] finding the path

2. <u>Looking Within</u>
[ ] discovering how it is with you
[ ] discovering what you want and don't want
[ ] recognizing your inner obstacles

3. <u>Activating Your Senses</u>
[ ] realizing that senses can be used negatively or positively: to harm through over stimulation, or heal and protect through focused attention
[ ] exploring positive ways to use the senses

4. <u>Tuning Into Spirit</u>
[ ] becoming aware of the timeless part of yourself
[ ] understanding that Spirit is the essential healer
[ ] looking at the vessel that houses the Spirit

5. <u>Exploring Interdependence</u>
[ ] building alliances from positive strength and energy
[ ] being supported along the path

6. <u>Finding Reference Points in Nature</u>
[ ] understanding your place in nature
[ ] learning and practicing the lessons taught by nature
[ ] seeing nature as evidence of divine energy and purpose and aligning with it

PART ONE

GETTING YOUR
OPERATOR'S LICENSE

Chapter

1

BEGINNING

Recovery is the journey of healing that begins at the moment when one embarks on the path of awakening and self awareness. One begins to examine long held assumptions, and the process of change is begun. It should not be assumed that change will be a pleasing experience, even if it summons positive change. Also, recovery is not exclusively the healing of addictions, emotional scars or disease, but the broad, inclusive domain of experience that women encounter through significant life cycle events, such as abortion, miscarriage, menopause, aging, loss or depression.

I remember an occasion when I gave a talk to a group of women on the subject of healing and as I began describing this process one woman asked very simply, "How do you do it?" I was somewhat startled by the question and was only able to give the woman directions to the path, not a quick answer for how to stay on course and manage the journey. She wanted guidance for her first steps toward inner exploration. This book is for that woman and others like her who struggle to find their way through the perilous depths of that inner pathway to healing. Some hurts heal on their own without special applications, interventions or cures. When we look at a newborn's miraculous healing ability, this is especially clear. However, as we go through life, this miracle becomes less accessible to us.

"Newborn is growing rapidly and this growth is evident in its ability to heal. Today's scratch vanishes with the passing of a day. Newborn is aging and being renewed at the same time."
From "Cosmic Travels of Newborn"

The exercises of this handbook are intended to remind us of the ways to tap into the miraculous pool of healing energy that restores our wholeness and connection to others and nature. The guideposts for healing, self discovery and self acceptance are the abilities to (a) *look within*, (b) *activate senses,* (c) *tune into the spirit*, (d) *explore interdependence*, and (e) *find reference points in nature*.

You are invited to use this handbook to gain skill in finding and following these guideposts. No journey is complete without the proper equipment and preparation, and, because skill takes time to develop, the exercises in each chapter should be practiced as often as necessary to derive maximum benefit. In addition, you are encouraged to adapt and vary the suggested exercises to meet your individual needs. Keeping track of your progress will allow you to maintain the needed momentum, so consider keeping a journal.

There is a basic outline for the exercises. Symbols, materials, themes, and affirmations are among the devices used to create concrete experiences from which insight and understanding can be drawn. Review the format carefully to see how you might best use it. Remember, the purpose is to promote the healing process, self discovery and self acceptance. These devices can be considered the tools that are meant to externalize some of this process to make the journey less intimidating. You are encouraged to use the exercises individually alone, with a friend, or in a small group. The exercises are not intended to be a substitute for other forms of healing help, but to be used in combination with other therapies and treatments to create holistic healing.

The following is a blank copy of the format for the exercises. You can create, add or modify exercises offered in this handbook. In fact, you are encouraged to personalize the exercises to whatever extent that you find supportive of your process of recovery, healing or self discovery.

Sharon M. Cadiz, Ed.D.

TITLE:
THEME:
GOAL:
AFFIRMATION(S):

MOTIVATION:
MATERIALS/SYMBOLS:
DESCRIPTION OF ACTIVITY:

EVALUATION/FEEDBACK:

OTHER FEATURES:
[ ] QUOTATIONS
[ ] POEMS
[ ] LESSONS: "WHAT I HAVE LEARNED…"
[ ] NEXT STEPS
[ ] ADD YOUR OWN AFFIRMATIONS, POETRY, NARRATIVES, LIFE STORIES, PICTURES, ETC.

Chapter
2

LOOKING WITHIN

The next step in your healing recovery is to look within. Imagine that your belly is your symbolic emotional center and a 'container' for stored feelings. Ask yourself the following questions as part of your self inventory. Answer on a separate piece of paper, and don't expect to complete this inventory in one session. You may be able to complete the inventory in one session, but don't put yourself or a group under any pressure or judgment, if you don't.

SELF INVENTORY

Is your belly—
[ ] Full (of what?)
[ ] Empty (of what?)
[ ] Murky [ ] Clear
[ ] What does it want?
[ ] What does it need?
[ ] If it were a room, what kind of room would it be?
[ ] Is it comfortable and airy? ___YES ___NO
[ ] Is it crowded and congested? ___YES ___NO

[ ] If it is empty, are you comfortable with that, or do you need to fill it? ___YES ___NO
[ ] If it is full are you comfortable with that, or do you need to empty it? ___YES ___NO

Your body home—

[ ] What is the general condition of your body home? Is it in <u>order</u> and <u>balance,</u> or disordered and in a state of imbalance?

[ ] What do you think your body needs?

[ ] What do you think your body does not need?

[ ] Can you recall when it felt good to be in your body?

[ ] What was special about that time?

[ ] Is your body home in good condition and order, now, but in poor condition at other times? ___YES ___NO

Write three (3) things that would make you more comfortable in your body home

    1. _____

    2. _____

    3. _____

Gifts—

[ ] What are your gifts?

[ ] What were you born with that makes you special?

[ ] Name some of your special talents.

Qualities—

[ ] What are the qualities you would like to change about yourself?

[ ] What are the qualities that you would like to keep?

Fear—

[ ] What fears to you hold about your life? [ ] What do you worry about?

[ ] What are you saying "yes" to in your life?

Favorite Things—

[ ] Name your favorite color(s) season(s) scent(s)

[ ] What is your best memory of childhood? Are there times when you recall this memory?

  If yes, when?

[ ] What smells do you recall from childhood?

[ ] Which are associated with good feelings? Bad feelings?

Food and Money—

[ ] How do you describe your relationship with food?

Is it—

  [ ] friend [ ] foe [ ] acquaintance [ ] sustenance [ ] lover

[ ] How would you describe your relationship with money?

  [ ] friend [ ] foe [ ] acquaintance [ ] sustenance [ ] lover

Your Monster—

Little Red Box
(adapted)
Author Unknown

Oh, I wish I had a little red box
To put my good friends in.
I'd take them out and—
[kiss, kiss, kiss]
And put them back again.
Oh I wish I had a little red box
To put my new friends in.
I'd take them out and—
[hug, hug, hug]
And put them back again.
Oh, I wish I has a little red box
To put my monster in—
I'd lock the door and throw away the key,
And never let it out again.

WHAT IS YOUR MONSTER?

GUILT   JEALOUSY   UNHAPPINESS
SHAME   ENVY   PAST HURTS, PAIN
WORRY   SELF HATE   ANGER

NAME YOUR MONSTER, IF YOU HAVE ONE:_____

Peace and Contentment—

What do you hear in the stillness?

What usually motivates your sense of excitement?

Name the place where your mind is settled/comfortable.

_____

EVALUATE YOUR RESPONSES AND ASSESS THEIR MEANING TO YOU AND YOUR HEALING. WERE YOU SURPRISED? IF SO, BY WHAT? YOU DO THE INTERPRETATION AND FINAL ASSESSMENT:

Final Assessment—

List:

Qualities I have_____

Qualities I like about myself_____

Qualities I would like to change_____

Qualities I would like to have_____

Qualities that will assist me in my healing_____

Qualities that might be barriers to my healing_____

Refer back to your self inventory periodically to assess your progress, movement and/or growth. Realize that the things you describe will change over time. The inventory can be used at times of flux, transition, challenge or imbalance to determine some possible causes for the discomfort or need to change.

The exercises in this chapter are designed to help you focus on yourself. You become the author of your change.

TITLE:	<u>Belonging to Yourself</u>
THEME:	SELF
	To focus on you/exploring independence and self love.
	To examine what it means to be you.
AFFIRMATIONS:	I love me.
	I know me.
	I see me.
	I belong to me.
MOTIVATION:	I recall reading a story to my children years ago that told of a dog who belonged to itself. The children marveled at this pet without an owner. The dog cooked for itself, kept its own house and took itself for a walk... Imagine a person not defined by roles and relationships.
MATERIALS:	Mirror
	Paper
	Pencil
METHOD/PROCEDURE:	IMAGINE
	VISUALIZE

1. Imagine that you belong to yourself. What would that mean? (Not someone's mother, wife, partner, sister, daughter, just you)
2. Meditations: eating and walking meditations/find the quiet focus in these acts
3. Things to do with one—write them down and select three (3) favorites

4. Temporarily shed symbols of ownership and title that detract from your vision of what it is to belong to yourself rather than others (rings, jewelry, etc.)
5. Look at yourself in the mirror. Recite a list of your gifts into the mirror.
6. Take yourself for a walk.

EVALUATION/FEEDBACK: How did it go?

Did it make you uncomfortable?

Are there other things you want to try?

[ ] QUOTATIONS: "Resolve to be thyself and know that [she] who finds [herself] loses her misery." Matthew Arnold

"God hath entrusted me to myself." Epictetus

[ ] POETRY: "Thorns to Roses" and "Rose Woman" by Sharon M. Cadiz

NEXT STEPS:_____

Thorns to Roses

It was by the thorn that my life hung;
Ragged, worn, without promise,
Endlessly snagged and pricked.
And, then, as I nursed the scar
That injured most painfully,
I gazed outward to see that roses grew on the same bush.
I mused about the wondrous possibilities of the rose;
Its rich luxurious scent;
Beautiful form and life giving promise.
The tightly wrapped gift would, I found,
Unfold and become more beautiful at every stage,
So I put myself in the rose.
It shielded me while I looked inside.
It protected me while I removed layers of pretense.
It shaded me from the glaring light of revelation.
It filled my senses with pampered moments of self awareness.
It reminded me how to grow.
It gave me inner beauty, and it finally helped me to see myself.
I sank my roots deep.
I anchored myself in faith.
Sometimes waving in the occasional breeze,
But always standing—
Covered in dew and raindrops
Waiting for the Sun
Until at long last, I stood
Embracing the precious blossom,
Not the piercing thorn.

Rose Woman

The winter was harsh.
The ground allowed no holes for an easy ascent.
She almost went down,
But a Spring sun called to her,
Even though she had never felt its rays.
A cosmic faith made her try to go
Toward the warmth of its glow;
Erupting into being when forces would likely have killed her, but...
She came to be because she didn't know how to die.
In the light, we could see her thorns,
And we knew they helped her arise,
So when she pricked us, we knew why.
She was a tightly rolled bud of layered depth;
A colorful drop of nature,
A treasure I'll never forget.
Petals fell off
And soon,
Just as Spring threatened to leave,
She bloomed in the robust color of her undaunted struggle,
Reminding me that the kiss of Heaven and Earth
Produced her one day and gave her to herself.

TITLE:	<u>**Who you started out to be**</u>
THEME:	**SELF**
GOAL:	To build awareness of your true self and your life's purpose.
AFFIRMATION(S):	I am special.
	My gifts are special.
	I behold the complete vision of myself.
MOTIVATION:	Imagine waking up at the beginning of your life.
	How did you experience the world, your caregivers and family?
	What special gifts and talents did you have as a child?
	What made you special?
MATERIAL:	Old photographs or pictures that depict how you imagine yourself throughout the major stages of your development. Memorabilia, mementos.
METHOD/PROCEDURE:	Imagine.
	Visualize
	Meditate.

1. Write a description of yourself using recollections of your early childhood. If you don't have a memory of this time try to imagine and visualize what it might have been like for you.
2. Describe your special talents/gifts.
3. Describe the earliest goals and dreams that you can recall.
4. Start a journal.

5. Detail the goals and dreams that started earlier and still exist.

6. Note those that you've already accomplished and meditate on those successes. Breathe in deeply with open or closed eyes as you think of those accomplishments.

7. Select one goal or dream which you have not accomplished and list three (3) steps toward it.

EVALUATION/FEEDBACK: How did you do?

Were there any problems
remembering?

Was this difficult?

[ ] POETRY: "Fragile Teacups" by Sharon M. Cadiz

[ ] PROSE: "Sea Glass"

NEXT STEPS:_____

Sea Glass

Recall, if you will, the origin of sea glass. Once it was a whole bottle, in tact and functional; a container for some substance. Then, it is thrown into "the drink" where it is tossed and dashed about until it is shattered into the pieces that, with time, are weathered and worn. Finally, the pieces are washed ashore; the beautiful and varied fragments of glass.

Now, think of the many women who were born whole with functional capacities and strengths, containing the substance of potential. Then, they are shattered by some powerfully destructive impact. They cannot hold on to their contents and they are broken into pieces, and the goal becomes one either of simply surviving by staying afloat; or seeking to unite with the other parts, feeling incomplete until they can accomplish the chosen goal.

When you behold the fragmented pieces, in whatever stage of the journey to completion, you are urged to

Respect
Validate
Normalize
Help
Comfort & Give Hope
And express thanks because they did not give up.

Fragile Teacups

She started out a flawless treasure;
Gilt edged, porcelain and floral design;
Matching saucer to catch her spills.
Time passed and her gold slowly faded
And the flowers were rubbed away.
Then her saucer was broken;
Crumbled into the pieces that were swept out of her life.
She stands alone—
Chipped, glued, slightly mismatched against her former self,
But she is still here.
She doesn't always want to be, but she is.
I see her and hesitantly
Think about myself the way she is today.
Will I be a fragile tea cup?
Aged, well worn and tea stained by time,
With few surprises and fewer dreams;
With hours to fill
Like empty cups on the cupboard shelf;
With missing sensations—
Lost when the saucer was no longer there to rest upon,
To catch heated brewing passions.
What will fill me and make me complete?
How will I survive?
Returning to an emptiness?
Waiting for the final drink?
No.

TITLE:	<u>Reclaiming Your Confidence</u>
THEME:	SELF
GOAL:	To tap into the source of positive energy within you.
AFFIRMATION(S):	I reclaim my inborn confidence. I celebrate my life in creative ways. I am wonderfully worthy.
MOTIVATION:	Recall a time in your life when you were full of confidence.
MATERIALS:	Paper Pencil
METHOD/PROCEDURE:	Meditate. Visualize. Imagine.

1. Take a special time in your life when you recall having confidence and write about it as if you were making a current entry in a diary. (Today I felt great...")
2. Give the date and state what is important to you and what the source of your confidence is.
3. If you can't recall a time when you felt confident, use your imagination to picture what you think that would have felt like.
4. Hold this confident picture in your mind. Visualize it (see it in your mind's eye) and meditate on it with a relaxed focus. Slow your breathing.
5. Do something that you always wanted to do, but never dared. (It should be positive, productive and life affirming).

EVALUATION/FEEDBACK: **How did you do?**

Were you able to recall a time when

you had confidence?

How did you act? look? feel?

[ ] **POEM: "On the Verge" by Sharon M. Cadiz**

[ ] **NEXT STEPS:**_____

On the Verge

I don't want to take better care of
My house than myself anymore.
I want to love my husband with
Passion as compelling as the ocean's waves.
I don't want to expect that
My daughter will want to clean the house,
Except for her own peace of mind.
I want her to love herself more than dust,
And to love her home only on the way to loving herself.
I don't want to labor without purpose,
And fold myself into each day
As another changeless ingredient.
I want to mine each day for beauty
And magnificence, and leave a jewel
To be strung into the necklace of my life.
I don't want to speak English
With its sharp corners and narrow meanings
As much as the poetry that is my life.
I want to be fluent in soul truth to
Liberate me from the prisons erected to house my spirit.
I don't want my son to be maimed by
Fear that makes him hurt others for sport.
I want to see my son enter that place
Where his truth and light will lift him
And shield him from the tyranny of pettiness.
Today I will have what I want and be
Beautiful in all I express.
Today I will be me.

TITLE:	<u>My Monster</u>
THEME:	SELF
GOAL:	To explore past hurts (psychic or physical) and begin to build the awareness to heal and manage the monsters that plague you.
AFFIRMATION(S):	I choose to be free right here, right now.
	I am not a victim.
	Fear has no power over me.
MOTIVATION:	Sing "Little Red Box."
	Make up your own melody for the song.
MATERIALS:	Drawing paper
	Pencil.
	Crayons in Assorted Colors
	Playdough or clay (Optional)
METHOD/PROCEDURE:	Breathe.
	Imagine
	Visualize.
	Listen.
	Meditate.

1. Make a picture or clay sculpture of your monster.
2. Describe your monster in writing with as much detail as you can.
   (What kind of power, appearance, etc. does it have?)
3. Determine what will banish your monster.
4. Ask yourself, do you want to be rid of it, or has it become a trusted companion.
5. What could replace your monster?

EVALUATION/FEEDBACK: How did you do?

Do you have more than one

monster?

Do you believe that you can

banish your monster?

[ ] **POEMS:** "Fear Is a Night Bird" and "Anxiety" by Sharon M.

Cadiz

[ ] **NEXT STEPS:**_____

Fear Is a Night Bird

Fear is a night bird—
Living in the shadow of day
And the hours before dawn,
Seeking the prey of your darkened gloom;
Searching between the creases of a wrinkled brow,
Under the stones in a heavy heart,
Swooping, spying the slightest patch of doom to feast upon.
The digital clock signals the arrival upon the backdrop of blackness.
The piercing claw clutches that gnawing pain,
Deep inside where no one sees.
There is no defense;
No guard to warn or shield against the attack.
Waking to the luminous wash of the sun's rays,
You look through the crumpled sheets
To find the menacing bird among the remains of the struggle.
You crawl out to find your way
Through yet another day;
Searching for how to banish the bird.
Then a sudden thought brightens the day
And the passages become lighted;
Remaining as such until the eyes close in slumber.
The bird hovers over your bed,
But cannot penetrate the beaming presence of peace.
It flies on in search of other food
And you awaken to the blessings of joy.

Anxiety

Gut wrenching, twisting, uneasiness.

Cork screw moods winding me into knots.

Stop it!

Cease the whining and be still.

Don't borrow woes to spill

Over into this new day.

Release your grip

And you will be shown the way.

Chapter

3

ACTIVATING YOUR SENSES

Our senses are the tools that guide and protect us in the world. Without them, we cannot connect with the world, or defend ourselves from the threats and dangers that can harm us. When one is self destructive through the use of drugs, food, relationships, etc. the tendency is to control and distort sensation to serve the self destructive purpose; stimulating or dulling to extremes. Distortions can be used to control what seems out of control. The exquisite balance and purpose of sensory experiences are lost under these circumstances; hence, the journey of recovery must be a quest to return the senses to their proper functioning.

Focus on choosing the positive sensations for your healing recovery:

FAVORITE—

*Color*_____

*Scent*_____

*Sight*_____

*Touch*_____

*Taste*_____

Sit in a quiet room alone. Select a particular color, scent, sight, taste or touch to visualize and experience with your imagination. In a mindful way, experience each fully and completely. The same exercise can be done with actual items or symbols such as cloth, perfume, photos, a poem, fruit, etc.

The following exercises will assist you in developing mastery in focusing on and activating your senses to support your healing and self-awareness.

TITLE:	<u>**The Ritual Bath**</u>
THEME:	SENSES
GOAL:	To restore senses to their purpose and heal them of past hurts.
AFFIRMATIONS:	I am clean.
	I am refreshed.
	I am renewed.
	I am new.
MOTIVATION:	In the quiet safety of your bathroom, affirm to wash away past hurts and to cleanse wounds in a scented bath. Think about the sensations. Cleansing can be thought of as a function of the inner and outer body.
MATERISALS:	Pine scented bath salts (or your personal favorite)
	Sponge or loofah
	Candle and holder
	A favorite colored plush towel
METHOD/PROCEDURE:	Meditate
	Visualize.
	Imagine.

1. Visualize yourself in a mountain stream.
2. Imagine that you are experiencing the sights, sounds, feel and smell of the mountain stream.
3. Focus and Meditate: Affirm that when you emerge, you will leave behind past hurts.
4. Watch the water and imagine the hurt and pain going down the drain.

5. Emerge from the bath renewed and refreshed for a clean start.

EVALUATION/FEEDBACK: How did it go?

Did you change the exercise?

Did it work for you?

Do you need to do it again?

Think about doing it over a week/month.

[ ] QUOTATIONS: "They that sow in tears shall reap in joy." Psalms 126:5

"Truth keeps the hands cleaner than soap." Nigerian proverb

[ ] POEM: "Mama's Kitchen" by Sharon M. Cadiz

[ ] NEXT STEPS:_____

Mama's Kitchen

Countless dishes took their bath.

Sudsy baptism for the plates upon which her family ate.

She hummed and moved shoulders up and down

To the rhythm of her life,

While looking out of her beloved window.

Across the world a gaze

To catch the outside reaches of her universe.

TITLE:	<u>Tea Ceremony</u>
THEME:	SENSES
GOAL:	To use a symbolic way to see the value and meaning in your life through use of the senses.
AFFIRMATION(S):	I feel my life.
	I smell my life.
	I taste my life.
	I savor my life.
MOTIVATION:	Describe your life in a word. Write down an adjective.
MATERIALS:	Chinese tea cup (no handle)
	Green tea
	Tea pot
METHOD/PROCEDURE:	Meditate.
	Imagine.

1. Perform the steps in the procedure in a thoughtful, deliberate way.
2. Prepare a pot of green tea/preferably from loose leaves (not tea bags)
3. Pour the tea into the cup; passing it through a strainer.
4. Pick up the cup with your hands around it. Sip slowly and smell, taste, and feel the tea.
5. Imagine the tea is your life. Mild to the taste, warm and comforting.
6. Take it "straight" (no sugar or honey to sweeten it)

EVALUATION/FEEDBACK: How did it go?
Did you want more sweetness or spice?

Was it too hot, or not hot enough?

How did it feel to hold your life in your hands?

See if you can find another symbol for your life.

[ ] QUOTATION: "Life is the childhood of our immortality."

Johann Wolfgang von Goethe

[ ] POEM: "Bring the Feeling Back" by Sharon M. Cadiz

[ ] NEXT STEPS:_____

Sharon M. Cadiz, Ed.D.

Bring the Feeling Back

The woman yelled,
"Help, I can't feel my life.
Where have all the sweet dreams gone?
The sensuality of sun on my skin;
The brief, but potent glimpses of joy;
The magical deliverance from pain;
The rain washed moods summoning summer love;
Dragonflies racing through my daydreams?"
I replied,
"Take off your shoes.
Walk toward the sun. Leave your umbrella home.
Send your line into the lake,
And wait.
Wait until the ground caresses your feet;
The sun kisses your arms up and down;
The rain washes you inside and out;
And there is a nibble on your line.
Open your eyes and you will see it all.
Open your heart and you will feel it all.
Finally, use this page to wipe your tears
'Til the feeling comes back.

TITLE: <u>**Hearing Voices**</u>

THEME: SENSES

GOAL: To make new inner "tapes" that support your emerging self esteem.

AFFIRMATION(S): I am...

I am strong.

I am brave.

I am beautiful.

MOTIVATION: Are there any old "tapes" from the past that you hear when you are fearful, afraid worried or angry. What do they say? "You're not smart enough. You'll never be able to do that. You're worthless, lazy, cheap," etc

MATERIALS: Voice recorder

Paper

Pencil

METHOD/PROCEDURE: Listen.

Imagine.

Visualize.

1. Imagine you as your ideal self.
2. Visualize what you look like and how you act.
3. Spend a few minutes formulating a list of ten (10) positive messages to yourself.
4. Prepare the voice recorder and save your messages. You may want to have background music playing softly.
5. Play your voice recording back.
6. Decide how often you want to play the tape.
7. Select a time when you will be uninterrupted.

EVALUATION/FEEDBACK: How did it go?
Did you have trouble writing?
Did you have trouble saying the
messages?
How would you describe your
voice quality?
Was it tentative, shaky, steady,
strong?
If you didn't like it, re-record it.

[ ] QUOTATION: "True enlightenment is lightening up on
yourself."
Cindy Francis <u>Life Lessons for Women</u>

[ ] POEM: "I Never Heard My Own Voice" by Sharon M. Cadiz

[ ] NEXT STEPS:_____

I Never Heard My Own Voice

I never heard my own voice and now you play it back to me
And I listen carefully.
In my voice I could hear that I was never heard
Never seen
And far from where I should have been.
Lost and trying to find my way back
To a place I didn't know—to a time that's not exact.
Heartsick and sad, I passed the time wandering corridors of emptiness
And then, I heard my own voice.
I had something to follow and it led me just beyond the wall.
It opened a door for me.
It loved me unconditionally;
Speaking comfort to a weary traveler.
And if I am fearless,
I can be reborn in this echo;
This vibration of life,
Or I can go the other way and dive from the highest cliff of emotion
Into the sea of despair.

TITLE:	<u>Bitter and Sweet of Life</u>
THEME:	SENSES
GOAL:	To experience bitter and sweet qualities in a symbolic way through the senses.
AFFIRMATION(S):	I savor the good in my life.
	I enjoy the different qualities of my life.
	Each moment and experience has value in my life.
MOTIVATION:	Think about a "bitter" experience in your life.
	Think about a "sweet" experience in your life.
	Write these down.
MATERIALS:	Grapefruits
	Oranges
	Paper
	Pencil
METHOD/PROCEDURE:	Meditate.
	Relax.
	Imagine.

1. Cut the fruit into sections and place on one plate.
2. Sample one fruit at a time (orange, then grapefruit).
3. Think to yourself: The sweet experiences of life are like the orange. The bitter, like grapefruit, can symbolize that which is not easy to like or enjoy.
4. Imagine that the grapefruit, like the orange, leaves "seeds" of like experience to grow in you, and nourish you.

EVALUATION/FEEDBACK: How did you do?

Did you have difficulty thinking of bitter experiences?

Do you avoid, dislike or forget about the "bitter" in favor of the sweet?

[ ] QUOTATIONS: "Each human life will eventually be fulfilled by a world of bitter and sweet dreams." Sri Chinmoy

"Patience is the mother of all change." Sharon M. Cadiz

NEXT STEPS:_____

TITLE:	<u>**Polishing Brass**</u>
THEME:	SENSES
GOAL:	To uncover the "new" you in the "old" you.
AFIRMATION(s):	I can remove surface tarnish.
	I can shine.
MOTIVATION:	Think of the "tarnish" that obscures positive areas of your life.
	Look through your closet, jewelry box or a "junk" drawer and ask yourself, "How much does my life look like this closet, jewelry box "junk" drawer?
MATERIALS/SYMBOLS:	Tarnished brass or silver
	A rag
	Metal polish or toothpaste
METHOD/PROCEDURE:	Imagine.
	Visualize.
	Breathe.
	Meditate.

1. Gather some tarnished brass or silver.
2. Keep one object or side tarnished, and polish the rest.
3. Think deeply about how areas of your life might resemble the tarnished brass or silver.
4. Begin to apply metal polish or toothpaste. (Toothpaste might be more available and can be used as a mild abrasive to polish the metal).
5. Breathe and relax your shoulders and hands and rub away the tarnish.

6. Contemplate how your special care produces a "new" appearance and compare this to the "tarnished" areas of your life.

EVALUATION/FEEDBACK: How did it go?

"What have you learned?

Did you relax with this task?

Do you have another way to activate your senses in your healing?

NEXT STEPS:_____

Chapter
4

TUNING INTO SPIRIT

Awakening to the spirit in you, as mirrored in your appreciation of your senses, nature and environment, as well as friends and companions, is a broadening experience. Spirit, in essence, is an expanding life force, opposed to the contracting, convulsive force of disease, addiction, or emotional trauma. Spirit is the animating force of being that is transformed, but never destroyed. Spirit is self renewing and eternal. The dragonfly, river, tree, newborn and grandmother are all imbued with Spirit.

When we awaken to our spiritual nature, the first lesson, and perhaps the hardest is *trust*. It requires that we trust an inner source of knowing that defies humanly fashioned rules of conventional logic and linear thinking. Some refer to the extension or generalization of Spirit as universal order, the manifestation of Spirit as it is made known to those who learn to trust the self correcting nature of the universe.

- It is in the changing seasons; the timing of birth; tides and cycles of the moon.
- It is the feeling that keeps you from stepping in front of a car when your mind is occupied elsewhere.
- It is the acknowledgement that things, both good and bad, happen for a reason.

- It is the faith or understanding that allows one to be content with knowing that some things remain a mystery.
- It enables one to embrace the paradox of life and death found in birth.
- It helps you to reconcile the understanding of "saints" and "sinners."
- Finally, Spirit is activated in you when you let go and surrender to the unpredictable guidance that acts in accordance with universal order.

I recall being in a park on a sultry summer evening and seeing two people dancing under a shade tree, mirroring the ease of nature; swaying like the leaves of the tree in the breeze. That was a manifestation of Spirit. Such an act is evidence that something exists beyond flesh, blood and intellect; something that can fuel a weary mind and body summoning another array of facilities that represent the domain of Spirit. Similarly, the frail elderly often take to the dance floor, in response to familiar music, with the poise and energy of youth; therefore, defying the limitations of time. Spirit is timeless, and there are no special time limitations; therefore, we can summon it at all times, and in all places.

Spiritual experiences connect us to the universal order, enhancing our lives because they help us to know more about ourselves and our path in life. Spirit is our most important guide to the path of healing, recovery and self discovery.

TITLE:	<u>Let Your Little Light Shine</u>
THEME:	SPIRIT
GOAL:	To uncover your gifts and show your radiance.
AFFIRMATION:	I seek the light of my being.
MOTIVATION:	Do you remember the song lyric, "This little light of mine,
	I'm going to let it shine…"
	Do you recall the saying: "Don't hide your light under a bush."
	<u>Note</u>: Don't force, *let* your light shine. "He [she] who tries to shine dims his [her] own light." Tao Te Ching
MATERIALS:	Candle and holder
	Matches, or
	Lamp with a yellow bulb
METHOD/PROCEDURE:	Meditate.
	Visualize.
	Listen.

1. Darken the room.
2. Meditate in silence, focusing on your gifts.
3. After a few minutes, focus on a single gift.
4. Light the candle or lamp with the intention to bring your gift into the light.

EVALUATION/FEEDBACK: **Did you have difficulty**
focusing on your gifts?
Did you feel uncomfortable?
What have you learned?
[ ] POEM: "Womanhood" by Sharon M. Cadiz
NEXT STEPS:_____

Sharon M. Cadiz, Ed.D.

Womanhood

Womanhood
Is a strange gift;
Mingling creation and being
Among the dried flowers of youth.
It is the reawakening to sensual pleasures
That restore newness.
It is the longevity of Spirit
That abides in peace.
It is the whisper of mind
That used to be chatter.
Womanhood
Is the gift we give ourselves.

TITLE:	<u>Forgiveness</u>
THEME:	SPIRIT
GOAL:	To free your Spirit of the oppression of past hurts and distrust.
AFFIRMATION(S):	I forgive now.
	I am free in this moment.
MOTIVATION:	How will you free yourself of those who have hurt you in the past?
	How will you release the villain in your past?
MATERIALS:	Empty plastic or paper bag.
	Paper
	Pencil
METHOD/PROCEDURE:	Imagine.
	Visualize.
	Meditate.

1. Imagine yourself taking control of unpleasant memories of people in your past.
2. Enlist the help of those who have been positive forces in your life. If you don't have anyone who fits this description, simply imagine a kind person and visualize how they look and act.
3. Visualize yourself in the role of "Healer of Past Hurts." Be playful and relaxed.
4. Think about a particular person who hurt you.
5. Write the person's name on a piece of paper.
6. On the other side of the same paper write the word _forgive_.
7. Put the piece of paper in the bag.

8. Blow air into the bag and trap air inside to make the bag look bigger.
9. Tightly close and hold the bag's opening, then hit it firmly and deflate it with a bang.
10. Sit in silence and take three deep cleansing breaths.

EVALUATION/FEEDBACK: Can you think of a better way to forgive and forget?
Are you willing to try it?
Did this exercise help you to release the pain and forgive?

NEXT STEPS:_____

TITLE: Let it Be
THEME: SPIRIT
GOAL: To practice being.
AFFIRMATION: I AM.
MOTIVATION: Describe three (3) places where you can focus
                     on just being, not doing.
                     Define non-action for yourself.
MATERIALS: Stones and/or shells
METHOD/PROCEDURE: Breathe deeply.
                     Meditate.
                     Relax.
                     Imagine.
                     Visualize.
                     Listen.

1. Sit in a comfortable place.
2. Remove yourself from any distractions such as telephone, television or radio.
3. Take three (3) deep breaths (one each for Mind, Body Spirit).
4. Become still and meditate on your breathing.
5. Relax your body (lower your shoulders, relax your face and hands).
6. Place the stones and or shells in the center of the floor.
7. Imagine that you are the stones/shells; motionless and expressing your essential nature.
8. Visualize yourself in peaceful stillness.
9. Place your hands in a prayer position and bow your head to your heart.
10. Close by thinking about non-action and the benefits.

EVALUATION/FEEDBACK: How did you do?

Was it hard to be still?

Did you find any benefits in just being?

[ ] QUOTATION(S): "To do nothing at all is the most difficult thing in the world, the most difficult and the most intellectual."

Oscar Wilde

"Ordinary riches can be stolen, real riches cannot. In your soul are infinitely precious things that cannot be taken from you."

Oscar Wilde

[ ] POEM: "More Than Fruit"

NEXT STEPS:_____

More Than Fruit

Slim, fruit bearing limbs,
Swollen with the fullness of Spring.
Sudden awakening,
Supple flower.
In season.
Wrapped and warmed by a will of twine.
Binding together all that she is.
Springs into her own,
Being stretched and molded.
Then puckered, pouting,
Sagging downward.
Empty fullness of a vacant womb.
Falling to the ground.
Landing on her feet.
Being the food for her own thoughts.
Sauterne of the soul.
New Woman...
More than fruit.
(Not just for tasting anymore).

TITLE:	<u>Making a Sabbath</u>
THEME:	SPIRIT
GOAL:	To find the time for spiritual respite.
AFFIRMATION(S):	This is the day of my rest.
	I will not carry heavy burdens this day.
	This is the appointed time to rest my weary Mind, Body and Spirit.
MOTIVATION:	Think of how you were taught about the Sabbath as a child.
	What did it mean to observe the Sabbath?
	How did you feel about it then?
	Do you observe the Sabbath now?
	How many days a week do you work (in the home or outside)?
	When do you rest? How do you rest?
MATERIALS:	Calendar.
	Marker.
	Paper.
METHOD/PROCEDURE:	Imagine.

1. Look at the activities of your week, both at home and out of the home.
2. Next, take a calendar and mark a day as the "Sabbath," your special day of rest and reflection.
3. Draw a line down the center of your piece of paper. Write down the things you will and won't do on your Sabbath.
4. Talk to your friends and family about this special day.
5. After you've observed your Sabbath, decide if you want it daily, weekly or monthly.

EVALUTION/FEEDBACK: How did you do?

Did it help you focus on *being*? your *Spirit*?

[ ] QUOTATION: "Things arise and she lets them come;

Things disappear and she lets them go.

She has but doesn't possess,

Acts but doesn't expect.

When her work is done she forgets it.

That is why it lasts forever."

<u>Tao Te Ching</u>—Lao Tzu

(translated by Stephen Mitchell

[ ] POEM: "Future Tense" by Sharon M. Cadiz

NEXT STEPS:_____

Future Tense

Tomorrow I will rest my mind.
Tomorrow I will take my time.
Walk the pathway to the lake,
Never a quickened step to take.
When I speak and when I breathe,
The air of peace will give me leave.

Chapter
5

EXPLORING INTERDEPENDENCE

Choosing friends should enhance and enlarge a positive vision of yourself. Finding positive friends supports your healing, strengthening and growth. Role models and mentors can be male or female, and the work that comes out of your own self exploration can clarify good choices for friendships and alliances. If you find within yourself a strong motivation to pursue advancement on a career path, you may want to select an effective, high profile male or female executive to emulate. If you aspire to be a homemaker and utilize your skills and talents on behalf of your family or community, you may find relatives, neighbors or other acquaintances to be acceptable role models.

In general, friendships should help you to feel more, not less self esteem, confidence and self acceptance. Also, friendships need not blind you to your faults or shortcomings; instead, they need to highlight pathways to you own self directed goals for accomplishment and positive transformation.

Often the experience of friendship is itself a process of growth and change. If it is not, it often begins to resemble role playing. You may remain the "quiet one," or "live wire" ever fixed in the role prescribed by earlier experiences, despite changing patterns, directions and needs. Such friendships can become stifling and destructive to life plans, self fulfillment, healing and growth.

Try the exercises in this chapter to create awareness about how you might think about friendships and other relationships, after you take this brief self inventory:

1. *Who would you speak to for encouragement, if you wanted to try something new in your personal or career life? Why?*

   _____

   _____

2. *How many friends, relatives or acquaintances support your efforts at self improvement?*

   _____

   _____

3. *Would you prefer to have more people provide you with this type of support? Why?*

   _____

   _____

4. *What kind of support do you need?*

   _____

   _____

When you have completed this inventory and reviewed your responses, use the exercises in this chapter to explore ways to allow others to enter your life in peaceful, positive and productive ways.

TITLE: <u>Fear of Friendship</u>

THEME: INTERDEPENDENCE

GOAL: To overcome the fear of friendships with women.

AFFIRMATION: Friends and foes are teachers.

MOTIVATION: Read the following:

"Faithful are the wounds of a friend,

But the kisses of an enemy are deceitful."

Proverbs 27:6

What do you think this means?

MATERIALS: Paper

Pencil

METHOD/POCEDURE: Imagine.

Visualize.

1. What would the perfect friend look like?
2. Describe this friend in terms of physical attributes and personality.
3. Draw a picture of this friend.
4. Does she resemble anyone who is in your life now?

EVALUATION/FEEDBACK: What are you looking for in a friend?

How do you suppose you could find such a friend?

NEXT STEPS:_____

TITLE:	<u>Jill and Jill Went Up the Hill</u>
THEME:	INTERDEPENDENCE
GOAL:	To support a friend in a common endeavor.
AFFIRMATION(S):	We succeed.

I am ready to embrace and accept the good that comes from togetherness.

Better together.

MOTIVATION: Read the following:

"Because of fear of rejection, some women endure dark pain alone.

"The silent hurts must be courageously exposed in order to find healing."

From: <u>Time for Myself: quiet thoughts for Busy Women</u> by Janet M. Congo, Julie L. Mask and Jan E. Meir

MATERIALS: Calendar

Small gifts

METHOD/PROCEDURE: Share.

Imagine.

Focus.

Plan.

Prepare.

Act.

Evaluate.

1. Select a project or undertaking that you and a friend might share.
2. Discuss what completing this project will mean to the two of you.

3. Focus your energy and imagination on thinking about how it could be done.

4. Make a plan and set dates on the calendar for completion of each sub-task.

5. Evaluate how well you did together in completing a challenging project *together*.

EVALUATION/FEEDBACK:

> Was it a successful endeavor? For both? For one of you? Explain why things turned out the way they did.

[ ] QUOTATION: "All who would win joy must share it; happiness was born a twin." By Lord Byron

NEXT STEPS:_____

TITLE: <u>Looking glass</u>

THEME: INTERDEPENDENCE

GOAL: To trust the positive vision of yourself reflected by your friend(s) and loved ones.

AFFIRMATION(S): I am worthy.

                    I am good enough.

MOTIVATION: Are you good at accepting compliments? If not, why not?

MATERIALS: Mirror

                    Paper

                    Pencil

METHOD/PROCEDURE: Listen.

                    Write.

                    Imagine.

                    Reflect.

1. Do this exercise with a fiend and record or write down the session.
2. Both of you will practice hearing positive remarks spoken each to the other.
3. Describe a positive trait or quality.
4. Write down the remarks you say about the other person and give them to her.
5. Do this for about twenty minutes, or until you run out of paper.
6. Gather the pieces of paper and store them in a special place for ready access.
7. Play back the recording or review the list at the end of the exercise session.

8. **Practice reading them to yourself in the mirror in the morning before starting your day.**

EVALUATION/FEEDACK: How did you do?

Were you uncomfortable? Why?

Why not?

What have you learned?

NEXT STEPS:_____

Chapter

6

FINDING REFERENCE POINTS IN NATURE

In your search for meaning and guidance on your journey of recovery and healing, find your reference points in nature.

"Study the teachings of the pine tree, the bamboo, and the plum blossom. The pine is evergreen, firmly rooted, and venerable. The bamboo is strong, resilient and unbreakable. The plum blossom is hardy, fragrant and elegant."
<u>*The Art of Peace*</u>
Morihei Ueshiba (Founder of Aikido)

Study how the tree stays centered and anchored while the branches and leaves move, swaying in the breeze. How much is that like you want to be: *sturdy, centered*; yet, *yielding, extended* and *flexible*.

Gaze at the river currents and how they react to the disturbance of the passing vessels. See the movement and interplay between water fowl, wind and reflections of the sun. Look at the birds and squirrels to see examples of living things full of purpose.

Enter nature peacefully and lovingly. Do not seek to dominate or control. Be an observer, admirer and soon you will feel very much a part of the harmony and beauty. In unity with nature, all relationships become clearer.

Learn the lessons taught by nature:

[ ] Go to an open hydrant, river, lake, ocean, stream, brook. Study the properties of water. (It doesn't run up, it runs down. It can wear away stone. It changes everything with which it comes into contact…)

[ ] Be aware of the changes of the seasons. Nature can teach you a great deal about change: how to adapt and accept.

[ ] Knowing how you fit in nature will help you not to feel like a misfit.

[ ] Your peace in nature is a birthright. Regardless of where or to whom you were born, or what circumstances in which you find yourself, nature will always accept you.

Use the exercises in this chapter to heighten your awareness of nature and your relationship to it, as well as learn the fine lessons that nature can teach you about resilience; renewal and rebirth.

TITLE:	<u>Finding Yourself in Nature</u>
THEME:	NATURE
GOAL:	To find out how you fit in nature.
AFFIRMATION(S):	I am a child of nature.
	Nature always welcomes me.
MOTIVATION:	Think of a favorite outdoor setting.
	What do you like most about it? Why?
MATERIALS/SYMBOLS:	Natural objects such as trees, rocks, river, sky
METHODS/PROCEDURE:	Imagine.
	Visualize.
	Reflect.

1. Take a walk in an outdoor setting.
2. Look at a particular scene.
3. Think of yourself as a natural object with which you identify.
4. Think about why you identify with that object.

[ ] **POEM(S):**   "Daffodils" by William Wordsworth

"Hope" by Emily Dickinson

NEXT STEPS:_____

Daffodils
By William Wordsworth

I wandered lonely as a cloud
That floats on high o'er vales and hills,
When all at once I saw a crowd—
A host of golden daffodils
Beside the lake, beneath the trees,
Fluttering and dancing in the breeze.

Continuous as the stars that shine and twinkle on the milky way,
They stretch in never-ending line
Along the margin of a bay:
Ten thousand saw I, at a glance,
Tossing their heads in sprightly dance.

The waves beside them danced, but they
Outdid the sparkling waves in glee:
A poet could not but be gay,
In such a jocund company;
I gazed—and gazed—but little thought
What wealth the show to me had brought:
For oft, when on my couch I lie,
In vacant or in pensive mood,
They flash upon my inward eye
Which is the bliss of solitude,
And then my heart with pleasure fills,
And dances with the daffodils.

Hope
By Emily Dickinson

Hope is the thing with feathers
That perches in the soul,
And sings the tune—without the words,
And never stops at all,
And sweetest in the gale is heard;
And sore must be the storm
That could abash the little bird
That kept so many warm.
I've heard it in the chilliest land,
And on the strangest sea;
Yet, never, in extremity,
It asked a crumb of me.

TITLE: <u>Sink or Float</u>

THEME: NATURE

GOAL: To sort through the "stuff" of your life.

AFFIRMATION(S):   I cast my burdens upon the water.

                    My sorrows disappear into the water's depth.

MOTIVATION: Think of the worries, burdens and heavy "stones" you carry in your heart.

                    Think of the surpassing joys that lighten/brighten your life.

MATERIALS: Sticks

                    Stones

METHOD/PROCEDURE: Imagine.

                    Reflect.

1. Plan a walk to an area with a body of water such as a lake or river.

2. Pick up sticks and stones along the way.

3. Think of the things you don't want in your life. Think of each of the stones as one of these.

4. Let the sticks become symbols of the things you want in your life.

5. When you arrive at the body of water, toss in each stone and affirm what it is you don't want in your life/things that you want to go away. Let each stone be that thing, then, throw it as far as you can into the water and watch it sink.

6. Think of what you want in your life. Think of each stick as one of the things you want in your life.

7. Toss the sticks into the water one at a time and reflect on the things you want in your life as you watch each float, ever present and prominently in sight.

EVALUATION/FEEDBACK: How did it go?

How did this make you feel?

Did you feel foolish?

[ ] POEM "In My Mother's House by Sharon M. Cadiz

In My Mother's House

She invited me beside the lake
To lovingly exchange some give and take.
I am reborn in her good grace
Once more to see my own true face.
I am certain to restore the peace
Lost in many days and weeks.
I feed the fish and sun myself.
Her living room is filled with wealth.
I remove my shoes not to spoil the splendor.
To the enchantment of her love I surrender.

TITLE:	Getting Grounded
THEME:	NATURE
GOAL:	To restore balance/stability to your life.
	To center yourself.
	To quiet racing thoughts.
AFFIRMATION(S):	I clear my racing mind.
	I get my Mind, Body and Spirit balanced.
MOTIVATION:	Visualize yourself as a young child, spinning wildly in a circle, then collapsing on the floor to still the dizzying movement.
MATERIALS:	A mat or towel.
METHOD/PROCEDURE:	Relax.
	Breathe.
	Imagine.

1. At a time of confusion or over-excitement, simply STOP.
2. Place your mat or towel on the floor inside, or on the ground outside.
3. Make sure that you will not be disturbed for about 15 minutes.
4. Lie down in a relaxed, flat position facing up.
5. Allow your abdomen to rise and fall with each breath.
6. Imagine that the floor is fully supporting you and giving you an opportunity to collapse in safety from the dizzying pace of life.
7. Return to this position when you feel rushed, confused or that your mind is racing.

EVALUATION/FEEDBACK: How did you do?

Did it work for you?

If it didn't, why do you think that is?

[ ] QUOTATIONS:

"In dwelling, live close to the ground,

In thinking, keep to the simple."

and

"What does it mean that success is as dangerous as failure?

Whether you go up the ladder or down it, your position is shaky.

When you stand with your two feet on the ground,

You will always keep your balance."

Both quotes from the <u>Tao Te Ching</u> by Lao Tzu

Translated by Stephen Mitchell

NEXT STEPS:_____

PRACTICE DRILL

Do a quick review with the following exercises.

MY MONSTER

Sometimes when we try to look inside, we find that a big, fierce MONSTER blocks the way. The MONSTER scares us away from looking at our true selves. The MONSTER is different for each of us. Draw and name your MONSTER. Some familiar names are GUILT, SHAME, ANGER, WORRY, RAGE, SELF HATE...you name it.

BELONGING TO YOURSELF

What does it mean to belong to yourself? How does that feel? Do you long to belong? Is it frightening to think of yourself alone and belonging to yourself? Can you think of things that symbolize ownership and title that detract from your vision of what it is to belong to yourself?

POLISHING THE BRASS

Think of the tarnish that obscures positive areas of your life. When you look through your jewelry box or a "junk drawer, does that remind you of your life? Tangled and tarnished?

PRACTICE BEING

Can you name three places where you can practice being, not doing. Think about non-action and the benefits.

SINK OR FLOAT

Think of the worries, burdens and heavy "stones" you carry in your heart. Think of the joys that lighten/brighten your life. Make the worries into stones and the joys or things you want in your life into sticks or twigs. Walk to the water and toss the stones and affirm the things you want in your life, and watch them float, ever present.

LOOKING GLASS

Are you able to trust the positive vision of yourself reflected by your friends and loved ones? Are you good at accepting compliments?

PART TWO

ROADSIDE TIPS

With every journey there are stops and starts; places to refuel and check directions. Now that you have gotten in some traveling time that has given you an understanding of the basic rules of the "road," you might need a little help staying on course. The following section is intended to do just that, creating space to test and challenge your capacity to handle the rough spots, following the guideposts and practicing how to use your "tools." You can ask yourself, "How would I handle this challenge?" "What course would I follow, if I found myself in a similar situation?" You can also derive some benefit from seeing how obstacles were overcome. You may have a different approach to your choice of life partner or lifestyle, but that should not impede your ability to draw understanding from the situations and lifecycle events that are described.

In this part, you will have an opportunity to glean some tips from a seasoned traveler. Adjust your rearview mirror, and fasten your seatbelt as I share what I have learned.

Chapter
7

WOMANHOOD: THE OLDEST PROFESSION

Proclamations on the road to a greater truth

I was born a woman to "father" a revolution and lead my people out of slavery. Not the slavery of chains, but the slavery of a spirit bound to the idea that forces us to prove we are helpless and hopeless in order to get a sense of support and connection. We are born into a helpful, interdependent, abundant universe, and our birthright is irrevocable, but negative forces convince us that we are individuals with no connection to a greater source of knowing and being. Feeling motherless and fatherless in a big world, we start to believe that this is true and we become orphans. As orphans, we are prey to every negative condition of mind, body and spirit. We are forced to see our worth only in terms of what we can do for someone else. We are forced to envision our purpose in the limiting terms of profit and loss; and we are enslaved by a life that cannot fulfill its promise. We are indentured to the belief that we can never pay off the debt that our birth established, so we must sell off parts of ourselves; little by little to survive, hoping that there will be enough of us to bargain ourselves through another day. We are charged for everything, so eventually we get down to trading in soul truth just to stay alive. Something like paying with our blood or tears for sunshine or paying a tax of suffering for rain. Sunshine and rain are ours and they don't belong to anyone of us exclusively. They *both* bring forth blessings that are ours to enjoy. But we become convinced that sun and rain are not ours unless we pay; and pay we must. Each of our lives has the promise of abundant blessings and we risk losing this endowment when we access the human forms of help that require us to give up the "deed" to our birthright just to get crumbs doled out in small parcels keeping us in the state of hopelessness and helplessness. Living this lie makes us *crazy;* then it makes us believe in lack and then it shows us that we are not worthy, and convinces us that our only salvation is in accepting that we are *broken* and *unfixable; unable to help ourselves.*

*   *   *

When I snap my fingers you will awaken from this sleep of the spirit and reclaim your birthright and begin to enjoy the blessings that are yours. However, because you were asleep so long you may not recognize yourself as a free human of divine origin. You may doubt that pure bliss and contentment are possible; that your every need and desire can be fulfilled. You may suspect that you will have to pay for every blessing with a piece of flesh or a sacred piece of your soul. That's why I am here, so that I can guide you into this new experience; so you won't be afraid or fall back into darkness. I was born a woman to "father" a revolution of spirit and to give you back to yourself. Open your heart and follow my steps to the threshold of your new address; and until you start getting mail there, you can use my post office box.

ROADSIDE TIP: Watch out for detours that send you down a treacherous, rocky road filled with mud and many hazards. Remember that you can choose the road for your journey, but you must have clarity about where you are headed and how you wish to travel. Above all, do not fall asleep at the wheel!

Chapter
8

DREAMING OUR WAY
INTO THE NEW REALITY

Leaving the Olde City for a New Destination

One night you dream that you hit the lottery and people start to notice you. They say, "Aren't you that woman who won the $200 million dollar lottery?" And before you can answer, they say, "Yeah, that's you," and they start to show you to the best seat in the place. They bring you a refreshing drink in their finest crystal and they never ask you for a credit card or cash to pay for anything…then you wake up and the rent is due at the same time that you misplaced your wallet that had your paycheck. Another day begins in the Olde City called Harsh Reality.

I'm here to tell you that this is not dreaming. The Olde City is the dream and your so-called dream is the Reality. You will initially doubt what I tell you and immediately look behind me to see if people are looking for me with a butterfly net and a straight jacket. I will stand steadfast and reassure you while staring into your eyes as though I see through the lies and confusion. I am prepared to tell you my story and further convince you that my words are true, so sit down, relax and listen as I tell the story of womanhood which is the story of every slave and whore that ever lived…the story of the oldest profession…

I was born by the river...the Bronx River. Brick and concrete were a backdrop for my cradle and I knew my parents before they were taken away and replaced with new ones called Need and Want. Because I knew my parents, I wasn't easily convinced that I was an orphan. Because they treated me as if I was a precious gift from an abundant universe, that memory sustained me through the long years of suffering that followed. This memory allowed me to believe that life was good and things could only get better and better with every breath. So I always took the time to look for that silver lining that framed the clouds, or the angel that dwelled within the seeming devil. My siblings were equally blessed and we lived in peace and tranquility for our early years.

One of my earliest memories is of being in my crib at night and seeing the shadows created by light breaking through Venetian blinds. Car headlights created a moving spectacle as the light raced along the wall, and that gave me my first experience of fear. Because I had no explanation for what I was seeing, I relied on a primal sense that this was a threat; something to be feared. This first fear created the precedent that made all unexplainable phenomenon possible threats to my sense of safety, and so the door to Harsh Reality was flung open and I nervously walked through.

If I were able to wake up, again, at the beginning of my life and understand that the images on the wall were not dangerous to me, perhaps I would have developed a different reality, but instead I was convinced that they would harm me. This was the beginning of helplessness. This was the start of a feeling that told me that I was powerless to ward off threats and dangers from without. Next, I surmised that I could not control this nightly terror, so I began to feel hopeless about my chances for escape. Hence, the twin demons of helplessness and hopelessness began their reign.

The scene changes and it is over forty years later when I had the strange sensation that I described as "awaking up in my life." I awoke one Saturday morning with an overwhelming sensation of peace and contentment that had nothing to do with my outer circumstances. It was a blissful feeling that was not altered by the events that transpired that day, or the changing events that unfolded. It was as though I was away for a very long time and I suddenly returned. At that time, this was not an experience that I was able to sustain for more than that precious day. However, the memory of it remained and I fashioned a new sense of my own reality from that tiny 'seed.' I realized that to have such a feeling created a new precedent and the potential for a new reality. This new reality was not based on fear, helplessness, or hopelessness and I was relieved.

Today the dream is the reality that I live. I ride the subway wearing a broad brimmed black straw hat in summer and a man says, "Aren't you somebody." I guess it's hard to conceal the fact when I woke up I gained the ability to project the appearance of what people think can only come from being a celebrity or a lottery winner. Live the fantasy and know that its not the clothes, lighting, or mistaken identity, but the result of transformation at the level of intention that creates your personal revolution. We are accustomed to living our fears and dreaming the fantasies we're too afraid to live.

Take my hand and I will guide you to where the day starts with the miracle that brings you back to life; and introduces you to who you started out to be. Everyone you meet will sense your presence as the truest form of human and divine expression…with or without a broad brimmed black straw hat.

ROADSIDE TIP: Don't mix up the street signs; pay attention and remember where you are headed.

Dressing in the Dark

When you wake up, remember not to dress in the dark. We often work at not seeing ourselves. We cloak fear and self doubt in the best or sloppiest clothes, excess body weight or in the meager cover of a starved body, and disguise our surroundings in the finest home furnishings or worst clutter to distract the onlooker from truly seeing us. Dress with the lights on to see yourself clearly and respect the fact that you are being birthed into a new day in a birthday suit that is as beautiful as you think it is. Others will usually agree with whatever your opinion is of yourself. If you hate the way you look, you can bet that others will hate the way you look, too. It's as important as anything else you do all day to dress the part of the beautiful person you are. The miracle is that you can be as beautiful in flannel and jeans as in Channel and heels. So, fearlessly open the shades or turn on the lights to see yourself and know that as you see yourself others will likewise see you.

ROADSIDE TIP: As you prepare for your daily trip, know that your underalls are as important as your overalls.

Food as Medicine

When we wake up we need a good meal. Food used to be medicine. The ingredients had healing properties; the power to determine outcomes, so they were used in spells and healing. Today, the vestige of this healing tradition is most clearly captured in our notion of comfort food. We know that a pursuit of this type of comfort can easily turn into overindulgence, so it is important to maintain a sense of balance and mindfulness about how we use the miracle of food. We know that if we eat enough food we can lull ourselves back to sleep; inducing a state of passivity that returns us to the condition of feeling hopeless and helpless. It helps us to know how to regulate our use of this miracle. Intention can change food from medicine into poison. Be sure to bless the meal with healing energy to restore harmony.

ROADSIDE TIP: Only make rest stops at places that serve the best food in ample, but modest portions.

Holding Your Breath

Waking up in our lives means that we reawaken to the miracle of the breath of life. It is the miracle that helps to make all other miracles possible. Sometimes without realizing it we stop breathing because we don't want to take in any more of the Harsh Reality, or we don't want to fill up with an inhale because we might take up more room and bring unwanted attention to ourselves; or don't want to let go with an exhale because we have learned to hold on to what's inside. Stop trying to regulate the miracle that regulates itself, and just let the breath flow in and out. Return to the state of both being aware of the breath and forgetting about it. Take a few moments each day to celebrate this miracle.

ROADSIDE TIP: Always check your exhaust pipe to ensure that it is clear for easy "flow" before each trip.

The River Speaks

The river speaks and if you take the time to sit and listen it will tell you its secrets. When you pause along the shore you will hear that water allows the river to stay alive. It brings in everything and the river keeps what it needs and moves on what it does not need. The water splashes on the rocks and we see, over time, that it can wear them down even though they are harder and seemingly more formidable. Even when people dump harmful things into the river, it can still live because water helps the river to move things on. If the river, as an expression of Mother Earth, endures and survives the insult of dumping because of the miracle to water, perhaps she is telling us that water is important to us as well. What we intend for the water we take in and use is as important as its purity and its life sustaining properties. This multi-purpose miracle can cleanse us and teach us not to hold on to the stuff that gets dumped into our lives. It can help us to let it go and see that as it goes down river toward the horizon, it loses its poisonous potency. Drink and wash in the miracle of water and you will be able to stay awake in the new reality.

ROADSIDE TIP: Travel the roads beside the river to remind you to how to stay on course and keep moving.

Healers

Many will claim to be healers and many will tell you that medicine will help whatever pains you, just remember that you are your own healer and you choose your own medicine. We are endowed with the same ability to heal as every other person, but because we may have been asleep, we did not realize it. Sometimes it is difficult to find the path of healing, so people who are aware that they are healers can help serve as your guides. When it comes to seeking remedies, if we learn to trust ourselves, we will find that everything we choose; be it a pill, totem, surgery, walk in nature, story or favorite pastime, can be our medicine. You will know it as your medicine because you have chosen it and it is your intention for it to be a healing force in your life. The simplicity of this idea may challenge your state of newly established wakefulness, but it can be gradually accepted if there is a desire to accept it. The result is that you will not be helpless and hopeless, but instead will take an active role in your healing.

We must bring back our midwives and medicine women and healers to assume a role for us in our pursuit of health and wellness. We need to think of the healing arts as an individual and collective calling that needs to be based on truth, love and intention. Modern medicine can be our truth, just like the ancient wisdom of acupuncture. What makes the difference is that true medicine it is administered with compassion, love and positive intention.

ROADSIDE TIP: Because you are going to be spending a lot of time on the road, be sure to seek the best mechanic and use the best fuel.

Undressing in Public

At the end of the day, know that healing from Harsh Reality can feel like undressing in public, and is met with about as much social acceptance. Healing within the context of our multi-dimensional lives can often leave us feeling that despite our efforts to cover and conceal, we have left some portion exposed, no matter how clever we think we are. When we hurt inside we learn to keep it to ourselves presuming that others don't wish to witness our process of releasing. When we think we have slipped and let on that all is not well within, we spend the night worrying what others may think of us. Intentional healing can, then, make us feel like exhibitionists of sorts, unraveling and uncloaking the unspeakable fears and pain that keep us prisoners inside ourselves. I am unlocking the cell and giving you the key to free yourself. And when you find a safe place and a trusted individual or group of individuals, you can take out the key, have someone watch the door and start *undressing.*

> **ROADSIDE TIP: Don't use public bathrooms at service stations, but wait for the better accommodations. (If you can wait.)**

Brazen Women

Women who are brazen enough to have dreams and a vision for their own journey of life are often labeled. Some of the labels would be flattering if one presumed that another's assessment meant anything. Other labels are cruelly negative and equally valueless and inaccurate. Being brazen means we have broken the chains of conventional thinking and forged a new identity based on the only truth that there is; namely, the soul truth that defined us as magnificent. And this is the moment that begins our journey.

> **ROADSIDE TIP: Vanity license plates give you the choice of how you want to be labeled, so think carefully about your choice.**

Women Warriors

Women who wake up are fierce. They are warriors who fight a daily battle not to succumb to the effects of being bombarded with the presumed role of the victim. The prize is another day without being buried by the expectation of our passive acceptance of lack, limitation and lovelessness. The woman warrior knows that she is never without, and she boldly walks in a forward direction even when she's tired of the struggle and weary of the journey. She goes on because an inner voice reminds her that not to live in the way of the warrior means spiritual death. When we wake up and prepare for our day like a warrior going into battle, we acknowledge that taking action is important to our existence.

> **ROADSIDE TIP: Prepare for the trip by getting aligned with the right directions and a *current* map. Some street names may have changed. Make sure you are not heading for the "Olde" City. Go directly to the corner of Dream and Reality and you will find them intersecting.**

Chapter

9

THE RANT

Oil Change

Now is a good time to share The Rant, so that we fully understand why womanhood is the oldest profession. The Woman will speak in the voice of her historic pain and no one is being blamed. We will share this story of pain and let it educate us. We will use it to support the revolution that turns on the axis of the head resting on the neck. It will move in and out of rhyme as it moves in and out to time; as we embark on the path of reason explaining to all, this change of season.

The Wage Whore

You tell me not to worry; you tell me just to rest, then point to a dirty clothes hamper and expect me not to fuss. You tell me about bills and money's evil demand that we work to keep it handy, then free it from our hands—to pay this bill or that and limit what we charge. You say work will make it better, so we don't become debtors.

I try to silence you with money to make the nagging stop; the fear and desperation speak sadness to my heart. I am the strong warrior woman, but and I can't ease your pain, so I simply hold my breath, get my purse and slowly go insane...

I'll be back on the street in a minute, just another corner and I'll get that check and bank the cash, I'll stretch the dollar to make it last I'll use my skills to make it more...lest you forget that I'm the whore.

The Shopping Addict

What sent you out there this time? A stressful week filled with sad anniversaries? What did you cop? "Toe thongs in multiple colors, books, a CD playing songs for lovers..."

I use plastic, if the paper is short. Needing more is how I get caught. Rummage through my purse for change, scratching like a dog with the mange. Today I walk alone without a stop, but I know that at any moment I might want to shop. I left the credit home to keep things cool, but credit acts like a friend and I'm its fool. Every addict has a dealer and if you've anticipated your recurring need, you have accounts at stores...yeah, you're hooked indeed.

The Beast of Burden

Would you take a finely tuned race car and use it to deliver newspapers? Loaded to the brim with heavy cargo piled within... I don't think so. So why would you take a magnificent creature of divine and human nature and subject it to the indignity of monstrous overload and other tactics just to negate her. She carries bundles, bags and such; always dragging; always too much. Up the steps, down the hall, balancing everything just not to fall. She's at the top and clears the stair, you open the door without a care. Just as she's ready to put everything down, it's time again to run all over town.

The Victim of Circumstance

I realize that I treat people like whole beings without missing or broken pieces and that puts me at a disadvantage when their perception of me is one of lack... When they see me as a fragment of their imagination.

The Scene of the Crime

I dwelled in hell and didn't know it. It took a walk back in to show it. I am made unwell by the sound and smell... Remembrances with stories to tell. The heavy burdens and the troubling tasks; punctured parachutes and broken glass. Bending spirit, breaking my back, brightened moments fading to black. Swelling the body with angry thoughts. Attitudes that were easily caught. Remembrances of bitter battles fought.

The Broken People

I know those who act like broken people.
At times, it feels as though I have a chest filled with them.
The accountant missing a part.
The artist fearful of making a start.
The dancer turned into a tart.
The writer who pushes a cart.
They walk around mumbling to themselves
About the treats they never had.
The sad misfortune that robbed their glee.
The broken promise; the missing key.
They want a change to descend on them—

But they want nothing to do with it until then.
Fold their hands,
Place them on their chest and let them await their moment of rest.

The 50 Ways

Fifty ways to say I'm sick and tired, hurt and hungry, achy, broke, depressed and "I want sex," and only one way to say, "I love you." The poverty of words is my inheritance, as a woman in the present tense.

The Holding In

Women are specialists in holding it in…so much so that we train our midsection to fold into itself…keeping the secret torment of life on the planet inside. But now midsections all over the world are breaking out. Our waists are larger and we don't wear girdles. The truth has begun spilling out.

Shards of Glass

I bought a candle at the store and when I went to light it I noticed that it was cracked. Not wanting to waste it, I lit it anyway and it burned just fine. As it burned down I realized that healing from trauma is a lot like the warm wax melting over the glass. If you're not careful you can cut yourself on the shards of glass embedded in the wax.

Mourning

I mourned her in the Spring
Reminded of the growing things
Then seeing the lilies and cars passing by
That is when I began to cry.
We'd sit for hours just to talk
Most times way past dark
And we'd laugh at jokes others didn't get
And keep our silences when others we met
We hatched some plans and shared some dreams
At times, we even listened to each other's screams.
You're gone now.
You left in the Fall.
Since going to heaven you hardly call.
But in the twilight of mortal night
I saw you in the half-remembered light
Standing there beside the lake
You declared that you had another path to take.
I recovered from that day
The tears came and washed the pain away
So when another sister
Loses a friend
I can tell her how our story ends.

ROADSIDE TIP: Avoid the road hazard of "black ice" that can cause you to slide out of control, focusing only on pain and panic. Respect it and know that it might be there, but don't plan your trip around looking for it when there is so much other scenery to see and enjoy.

Chapter
10

UNDERSTANDING THE MEANING OF LOVE

Love isn't like owning a car

I was nineteen when love arrived with a simple message directed to the beloved: "You don't have to *do* anything." Other suitors needed to arrive bearing gifts; a dashing look; a white convertible car; a beautiful smile or dark wavy hair. This one was different, not that he did not possess fine qualities, but because that didn't matter. He won my whole heart with his complete being. So odd this was that I wondered what had distinguished this one from the others. To know the answer I had to search beyond the temporal to the timeless. I felt a depth of feeling that spanned oceans, centuries and lives. If lost, I would find him again and again and always know him.

It was my custom to say to him, "You can go anywhere in the world, as long as you return to me," and he always did. I studied his nose; his hands and mouth and recognized them as the markings by which he was to me now known. I knew him, likewise, by the brooding stare rooted in worry and angst and by his active nature that made the doing of things a clever contrast to my pensive soul. I knew him by a manly scent that gave a primal quality to a loving presence. Perhaps I knew him best by an honesty that demanded expression in everything

102

from the return of a wallet found on the street to an inherent dislike of anything false or dishonest.

But love is more than all of these, and so as I swam in the depths of it, I found that I could pledge myself to be happy for his happiness, with or without me bound to it. This nature of true love surprised me most because one usually wants to attach to the object of love; to have it stay forever theirs. I stumbled upon this profound quality of love that knows nothing of geography or time and, therefore, does not reside only in a place or period; a lifetime or a locket, but is the unattached part of our inner spirit, benevolently keeping planets in their orbit, grass growing in Spring and women and men who have known it smiling on their deathbeds.

ROADSIDE TIPS: On the journey, there are many stops. One that is not to be missed is the one that takes you down a rose covered path to a fragrant meadow beside a brook where you will look down and see two reflections instead of one.

Chapter

11

THE COSMIC TRAVELS OF NEWBORN

Important Travel Log

S o it begins…

This morning the baby rumbled with life; like a lively hamster in a cloth purse. The soft, jittery, wave-like movements punctuate my momentary thoughts. I curiously think about the universal cosmic clock that chimes the hour for a new traveler to begin its journey to earth.

At fourteen weeks, I heard the baby's heartbeat. It was like listening to someone tune in an overseas channel on an old radio. The beat penetrated the static in a rhythmic thump. We were to have further radio contact in the coming weeks. The baby's location was charted somewhere west of my equator.

I sleep lots and ache even more. I give myself to long periods of rest while this tiny one plugs into my generator to refuel and energize. Rude reminders such as indigestion, headaches, backaches, weakness, leg aches and nausea alert me to the Time of Changes; the volcanic eruption of life. This is the critical time of testing. The tiny traveler tests the vessel and begins to fortify for the journey.

In the second trimester, I am the paradox of abounding energy and overwhelming emotional fatigue. I wake up crying because despite my high energy, I cannot do all and my wishes become cumbersome burdens. I yell too much and cry too much. In between, I accomplish amazing feats of daring—like a ten mile bicycle ride to see my mother. Doctor visits chart our progress and predict a safe landing, while I examine my stomach for signs of blooming. I sometimes send messages to my baby: "You're not going to hurt me, are you? Then I think, "Well, it won't matter; just get here safely."

I am the mother ship and in the third trimester I have become fairly global in appearance. The baby's leanings are marked on a road map of varicose veins just to the back of my left leg. The linea nigra has darkened and become a line of demarcation. The time slowly approaches. All must be made ready for the splash down.

I sit alone in a darkened room rocking in my chair or staring at a wall. I talk less and feel less like engaging in frivolity. The unity I've shared with my husband turns to a single minded drive to prepare for the coming event.

I sit in my rocking chair and cry a little. The tears are of joy and a deep longing to feel every sensation of this delivery with pleasure and excitement. I try to coach myself into the awareness I'll need to help this baby come into the world. I want to see the baby come out of me and know that we traveled together through time to arrive at this momentous rendezvous. This is my way of sharing this miracle and understanding it.

Fear is mingled with anticipation, as I stand at the beginning of a narrow passage into a dark corridor, which I must walk alone. When I sit in solitude I feel sadness and a desire to run away to a clean, green meadow and just having the baby there in the quiet. The comfort of my inner wisdom helps me to visualize peace and tranquility to balance my uncertainty and momentary despair.

Birth is an enormous paradox. With each birth, you die a little. As life emerges a void is left inside, an empty space that sinks deep, leaving a plot. Such a plot will reside in me, marking where newborn had been. The miracle; a timeless rite, is life and death; rejoicing and mourning.

The Morse Code of labor pains signals the impending arrival of newborn. Newborn's head is engaged in the chamber, and after hours will flow into the world. This may be the hardest part of the journey. The progress is measured in centimeters.

All the vital signs are checked and Nature presides over the event with the certainty of an ancient midwife. The moon/the tides/ the baby inside. We, and the Universe, synchronize our clocks.

The fetal monitor is attached; the I.V. is inserted and the countdown begins. The final passage into light begins. I hold onto an invisible pole that is slippery and rising up out of an abyss. I cling desperately with each jarring pain. To let go would mean falling into endless space. Relax and breathe; pause; release. I focus and relax to see that the "pole" is my husband's flexed arm within his wrinkled shirt sleeve.

Another tremor is forecast by the monitor and I begin to ride out the wave in pants and blows. Radar is now tracking the traveler right over the target. The canal opens and with light speed, we are drawn apart; connected, finally, only by a small rope and anchor. A protective garment of lanugo, which is worn in the womb, shows from the instant of birth a mechanism for survival which is an ageless wonder. Newborn rapidly employs the movements and gestures that are the survival tools we call reflexes. A great navigator must guide us into this cosmic space and teach us the laws to govern our travels. Sometimes the travel maps are lost or abandoned and travelers suffer through life instead of blossom through it.

I feel every inch of newborn as it emerges, being pulled out of my inner sea. The first part of the journey ends, and the awakening begins. Newborn is the world. The eyes are part startled; part curious; part knowing. The hand clutches a finger in a strange desperation. The arms wave as if falling from a high place; trying to fly, or swim, or crawl—struggling in a strange new medium: air. Is newborn a fish, bird, crawling creature or all of these things?

And then, Newborn is the world. It scratches its face, but doesn't know what causes the pain. Newborn is gratified by sucking a pacifier that is, then, snatched away by its own hand. The world causes its own pain, at times, and has the power to satisfy its own needs unless, like newborn, it stays ignorant of its role in the suffering.

Newborn is all eyes and intellect because sensations reach it there. Newborn is not arms, legs, torso, fingers, and feet; Newborn is head, mind and soul. Its head is its essence; the heaviest part of its being and the most fragile. Gradually, it will lift its head to see; turn its head to suck; lower its head to rest.

Newborn is a cosmic traveler brought here by a mother's prayer and a father's dream. At first, it fluttered its eyes in half sleep, dreaming of a former life; a life complete in every way. Now, we guide newborn through our universe and hope that it will help our planet flourish and grow. The dream will not die until the seed dies. I am the seed of my parent's dreams.

Newborn is a month old. At first, breastfeeding was painful and I counted the minutes instead of counting the stars, or toes on newborn's feet, or singing a lullaby. Finally, I nurse with ease. I read stories, sing songs and play silly games.

Newborn is growing rapidly and this growth is evident in its ability to heal. Today's scratch vanishes with the passing of a day.

Newborn is aging and being renewed at the same time. The miracle that brought this cosmic traveler continues.

At fourteen pounds, with bright eyes and an intense stare, newborn often breaks into a wide grin. Newborn is restless for stimulation: motion, new sights, and exercise of arms and neck muscles. Body movements like kicking legs and whirling arms propel it through the days that follow.

I write about newborn because it teaches me about myself. There is a newborn in each of us. Often when we discover it, we feel defensive, vulnerable, exposed. Newborn is the truth; the purity of spirit we have hidden beneath, safe and secure, but curiously the discovery of it can lead one to feel threatened and unsafe. We grow older, but little changed from our basic infant selves. Newborn cries for gratification—the longing for the Eden of the womb. It is soothed by a hand; a soft voice; a loving caress. We hear the cries mounting within us our whole lives through. Our lifelong cries bespeak our intimate knowledge of newborn.

Now, my family's solar system has changed its orbit, and the new arrival reorders our lives. There is little time for anyone else in this time of intense mothering and care giving. My attention is drawn to the fact that we are all travelers and new arrivals. My husband is one traveler in a slightly remote orbit around newborn. He must be experiencing a strangeness in our new patterns. He didn't directly feel the pain or *have* the baby; yet, we labored together to bring newborn here safely. There must be an emptiness; a strangeness that he can't connect with, although, like me, he must feel reward and a sense of loss.

I daydream of a mountain lodge…evergreen with fresh air that lifts you off the ground…a warm spot in a cozy room; radiating with colors that soothe and music that calms. We rest, then, awaken.

Peace is everywhere, if not in reality, at least in my thoughts. Perhaps my husband's daydreams are the same. Habits keep us going, but commitment keeps us whole. We remember the dance, but have temporarily forgotten the steps. I'm sorry. You trusted me long ago, and now I am not at all the same, except in the fleeting light of a sweet remembrance.

Newborn grows and becomes a creature of the world, instead of the world—no longer the face of space, but the arms, legs and moving parts of self. When awake, newborn shakes the world like a rattle, forcing it to give up its secrets. Asleep, newborn wiggles beneath the covers just as in the beginning, like a hamster in a cloth purse, and I think of my husband and the journey ahead. Perhaps soon we will meet again as we ramble the paths we once traveled together in daydreams—this time with the wisdom imparted by Newborn.

> ROADSIDE TIP: Relax and enjoy the ride. You can't fully prepare for this part of the journey, so just pack a lot of "Love" and "Patience." Make sure there's always sufficient gas in the car so you can go out and get more for when they are in short supply.

Chapter
12

OVEREXPOSED

How to get TLC out of GYN

I see stunned faces emerge from the dressing rooms clinging to the meager dignity of a flimsy examination gown. They hurry to a seat and await the next order from the stranger who bade them undress. Nervous anticipation takes many forms. Some women make jokes about the doctor's practice of having medical interns peer at a patient's "private parts." Others become enraged by the length of the wait and the short duration of the actual time with the physician. Altogether, they sit in waiting rooms appearing as damaged goods; the products of years of maltreatment at the hands of a well intentioned, but poorly administered health care system. It's not overstating the point to describe these women as victims whose shame is the product of another's insensitivity.

The women's liberation movement sent some of our 'kind' to medical school to represent our plight, but the system has transformed them into their male counterparts. Dressed in doctor's garb, some female gynecologists employ the same tactics that keep women ignorant about their health. They take blood pressure and don't tell the patient the results. They ask probing questions without explaining why. Too often, when a special procedure or treatment is needed they fail again to explain why.

Well, I've seen the last nervous woman I want to see! Today I saw a woman who could be my mother sitting in a small waiting area with others who were waiting to see doctors. She was embarrassed and a little ashamed of her appearance of uneasiness; ashamed that others would think it foolish to be modest...at her age. A popular phrase is, "we're *all* women." Yes, that is true enough, but something makes us feel vulnerable. Something makes us feel that even though we've had our sexual lives and babies, as women, we are not always comfortable with being probed and peered at by virtual strangers. These feelings complicate the notion that medical treatment is beneficial. Consequently, there is a feeling of ambivalence and uneasiness that can frighten and embarrass most women.

Many women report being made to feel that they should be grateful for what they get; especially when they attend clinics, or have certain forms of low end coverage. Of course, a patient's ability to pay is no reason to downgrade the quality of care, if one is truly practicing the healing arts. I, for one, am not grateful because I find myself victimized by a system that robs women of their dignity and their right to sensitive care. Often we are socialized to think that doctors know more about our bodies than we could ever possibly learn; yet, the value of a doctor, as I see it, should be measured by how well she succeeds in educating patients to understand their conditions, and supporting them in utilizing proper health maintenance. Instead, we find most of the physician's time is spent on treating illness, handing out pills, and scheduling surgery. If they can't cut it out, medicate it out; you are probably thought to be on your way out. Too many of us bought into this model in the worse way. Doctor's intimidate us and we accept it. Doctors try to educate us and we find another doctor. We cannot hope to end the operating room oppression or office visit jitters until we decide what kind of health care treatment we want. Ideally, women should be partners in their healthcare, not adversaries or subordinates.

After thinking about why some women are speechless in the presence of gynecologists, I finally realized that being told to enter an office, strip and sit all in the first few minutes of an examination puts the patient in a passive, subordinate role. As a result, it is difficult to speak intelligently about ones condition. The patient should be made comfortable in order to build a bridge of trust, but instead the patient is given a gown and an order. We should question the appropriateness of these practices because they reinforce a subordinate role for the patient.

The next time a doctor forgets to draw the curtain before she tells you to get undressed; fails to spend a moment on introductions or greetings, or assumes you're just too stupid to understand your own health needs, I want a universal scream to go out that will wake up all the medical personnel who practice medicine in their sleep. I want women to become their own advocates. I want women to rise up and end the two hour wait for the seven minute visit; the unauthorized studies of their bodies to further medical knowledge; and the condescending treatment that presumes ignorance. Let's do what Rosa Parks did—sit down and refuse to move when the seven minute visit leaves us limp with disgust. Demand recognition for our individual needs. Let's boycott unprofessional doctors and make sure a "change is gonna come."

We should also choose our doctors with as much care as we select a hairdresser. Certainly, we should be selective and when that is not possible due to prohibitive costs, we should demand high standards anyway. Finally, when a physician performs inappropriately according to the profession's best practice standards, or is guilty of misconduct, we have the responsibility to report the matter to a regulatory agency such as the Office of Professional Medical Conduct, affiliated with state boards of regents or licensing agencies. Remember the Chinese proverb as a standard of medical performance: "The Superior doctor prevents illness; the mediocre doctor cures imminent illness; the inferior doctor treats illness."

We must know that things will not change if we do not change. I intend to take charge of my next examination by keeping my clothes on and exposing my ideas, concerns and questions before my body.

> ROADSIDE TIP: Yielding the "right of way" works best when all parties observe the rules of the road. When we yield to poor treatment we are effectively condoning it. At some point, we need to put up a STOP sign.

Chapter
13

RED LEATHER PURSE

<u>Holding it together in stressful times</u>

Life and death are mysteries that inspire all sorts of thoughts and ideas that are themselves mysterious and lofty. Well, I have found that some of the best insights come from the simple things right at hand; and when I look to them, I see with the clarity of a crystal ball. My red leather purse was one such object that accompanied me for some important parts of my life journey.

My red leather purse saw me through the death of my mother; the birth of my first grandchild; a series of ego deflating setbacks and several depressing near misses. It opened up to welcome me inside its secret recesses that held candy wrappers that betrayed intentions to diet; the crumpled movie ticket stub and the thoughtful greeting from a friend. Perhaps more importantly my red leather purse, with its many folds and pockets, gave me a portable environment that held my stress ball, lavender aroma mister, inspirational quotations and a classic Hallmark greeting that read, "When things are bad and getting worse, keep a cookie in your purse."

When I had my red leather purse on my shoulder, I was invincible. I was Venus rising from the sea; the Earth Mother; the Harvest Queen; the Goddess; the Conqueror and the Storyteller. We are companions on the journey and in the right light I saw my purse as the truest symbol of my life. Like my life, the red leather purse held the contents of my days. It recorded the events and it supplied a "hanky" for the sad times, and confetti and party horns for the happy times.

Come with me inside this wonder of human invention and know the blissful delight of witnessing your journey just by looking within that small piece of leather with a strap. Know that the journey may have all manner of companions, but a purse will hold you up, keep you together and tell you things that a friend and family would never dare about what you really value. Look inside and learn.

> ROADSIDE TIP: Pack well and keep all the "essentials" close by. You never know when you will need them as you make your way down the road.

Chapter
14

MEDITATIONS ON
THE BLACK CAT

A tail of wisdom for the road

As I strike the keypad to tell my tale, I picture a Black Cat casually walking across without regard for my earnest commitment to staying focused on the task at hand. He strikes a series of 0000000000000's covering a line or two, and I then gently coax him off the key. He moves on to follow the warmth of the computer monitor around to a cozy spot toward the back where he curls up for a nap, as I continue to tap out my words. And there he rests; content that he has punctuated the moment with his indelible mark. I stare at the places where he sat and the keys that he tracked over only to realize that he is not there. The memory is a phantom reminding me that my great teacher is gone. The Black Cat, who taught me so much, is gone, but I am left to remember and share the lessons that he so generously imparted. You can be my audience as I unveil the mysteries of life revealed by a curious and mischievous character who retained his youthful vigor for all of sixteen years; and who reigned as the resident authority on how to live life to the full. I honor our friendship in the telling and re-telling of his exploits and adventures and humbly offer you the gift of meditations on a Black Cat.

Stay on Top of Things

Sitting in a comfortable position, poised and ready to work with papers piled high in front of you; taking your pen in hand as you are just about to start, the Black Cat jumps up onto the table and sits right in the middle of your work. This creates a quandary. What is the most important thing to do in this moment? Should you push him away and continue to work, or simply marvel at his indifference to your plan? Do you envy his special disregard for all things that resemble toil, or do you shake your head and complain about the creases he has made on your page. Indeed, he has taken your dutiful pursuit of efficiency and made it a comic catastrophe. Take a deep breath, inhaling to the count of three and exhaling to the count of three. Put down your pen and join the Black Cat in his state of blissful repose on the stack of papers.

ROADSIDE TIP: Always yield to the higher purpose of love in expression.

Learn to Tell Time

Some people use a watch to tell time and continuously consult their watch or the wall clock to know what time it is. The Black Cat with amazing accuracy and precision always knew the time. This was no stupid pet trick. This was one of the marvels that made the Black Cat such a gifted teacher. He would wake me up every morning at the same time. When I stirred from my room, he would be standing right there, as though air dropped from a low flying airplane. I always wondered how he knew when I would open the door. It didn't stop there. For sixteen years, every night when I returned home, he would be standing there as I turned the key and pushed open the door. With ninja-like skill he was there sitting majestically poised to greet me upon my arrival. Mastery of this skill comes from the stillness that stirs one soul to synchronize with another. It is the rhythm of lives in tune with each other. It is the church bell without the clock; it is the rooster at dawn and with solemn sacredness these guardians of time preserve Life's meaning by marking places in the day. To experience this, remove your watch and look away from the clock. Ride the gentle waves of the day's current with its ebb and flow, and let it take you to the moment of awakening and the time of arrival.

ROADSIDE TIP: Sometimes let the journey just unfold and let it take you off the path without a concern for time or being late. Some valuable treasures reveal themselves as you meander and get lost.

Know What Matters

He was black. I guess that would be all you had to say, but there was more. He had a unique stare; a way of looking that made you know that most things really don't matter. If it is rainy; if it is sunny; if you're miserable—none of it really matters. It wouldn't matter if you're angry because he threw up another hairball on the couch; or if he cried and cried for you to fill his dish; and if you stepped on his tail while stumbling around in the dark. He didn't get stressed if you were slow in filling his dish, he would simply keep reminding you. For every mood and every action, he would just look out at the world with an understated acknowledgment that he would live each day by his rules, engaging our attention for the simplicity of the moment that is forgotten the instant that it slips away. What mattered was that even when you yelled at him, or stepped on his tail by accident, he would hold no grudge; harbor no resentment. He would never remember a slight, but he would always remember to be there to give comfort through the long night of an illness or period of sadness. Knowing what matters means staring out at the wide world and not seeing it for what it does, but for what it is.

ROADSIDE TIP: Don't fuss about an itinerary that drives you to distraction. Put the car on cruise control and enjoy the ride, instead of worrying about the drivers who cut you off.

Put a Bell on It

The moments slip by so quickly, turning corners on two wheels while we fumble to find our cell phone in a purse; read e-mails with our lips moving; or stay awake worrying about what will go wrong. We ask, "Where did the time go?" "Is it Christmas already?" "I can't believe you're all grown up." My advice from a wise Black Cat is to take the moment and, like you would with an impish kitten that strays into mischief, put a bell on it. Then you will hear it ring and take notice of the passage of time. You will notice that Black Cat represents a piece of the divine. The bell will sound to remind you that he honors you with his loving presence as he moves about your home. The bell will say, "Hey, did you see that?" It will encourage you to see how the cat goes barefoot, feeling the floor on the pads of its feet. It will captivate you with the myriad possibilities for how you chose to breathe, sit, stand and spend that valuable gift of one single moment that ends almost as quickly as the bell when it stops ringing.

ROADSIDE TIP: Occasionally make some noise when you are ambling along. Raise the volume on the radio or give a cursory honk to accent the passage of time on your wonderful journey.

Be Purr-fect

Not everyone can be purr-fect. Actually, only cats can be purr-fect because they invented the art of doing all things in ways that they themselves find satisfying. Note that satisfaction does not mean satisfactory according to an external standard or measure, but according to the determination of the feline. The Black Cat was a purr-fectionist. He had a preferred way to be carried, and would be purr-fectly content to be carried about for hours at a time, if you had the stamina. In his purr-suit of self-indulgence, he was a supreme master; soaking up attention, pets and long naps in cozy comfort. You might ask, at what cost did he purr-sue such indulgences. Well, his lesson to me was that purr-fection was free.

ROADSIDE TIP: Be your personal best on the road of life and most times for most people, including yourself, that will be just *perfect*.

Share Your Food

Full plates beg the question, "Can you really eat all that?" The Black Cat gave the answer to that question saying with an audacious stare, "No, you better share." When you were slow to respond, he would jump onto the table, challenging the rules of etiquette in a desperate effort to save you from yourself. When that didn't work, he would weave around your chair signaling that time was passing. Next, he might come to a seated position poised where you could see him, reminding you that patience is a virtue. Before long, this princely messenger would walk away turning his back on your indifference and concluding with the wave of his tail that gluttony is its own punishment.

> **ROADSIDE TIP: Don't be a "road hog." Taking to the road to dominate the experience will keep you always craving more and not feeling like there is ever enough. Sharing the road and your life can make the trip a lot more interesting.**

Take a Nap

You haven't truly napped until you've done it with a cat. Pardon the rhyme, but it's about that time…Okay, enough. When it's naptime, most people decide to gulp some coffee instead because there's work to be done. The Black Cat would awaken in the morning; have his breakfast; accompany me from room to room as I prepared to leave; take a quick run through the apartment playing "tiger in the grass," then retire to a bed, chair or sofa for his first nap of the day. As I would leave, the sight of him resting made me envious beyond words. On some mornings, he would accompany me to the door to lessen the sting of his enviable advantage. The institution of the nap was practiced by the Black Cat with the discipline and abandon characterized by an effortless retreat into the highest state of meditative mindfulness. Each nap was a masterpiece of healthy detachment and peaceful relaxation the likes of which generally evade those of the human persuasion. Humans indulge in the practice of feeding a cold; starving a fever; and plowing through the hours of the day intended by nature to provide what one researcher refers to as the "sleep pressure" that invites us to nap. Another favorite way that humans ignore this basic need is by chomping down cookies, cakes, candies or lattes to relieve the feeling of tiredness that threatens productivity. Simply put, just watch a cat and take a nap.

ROADSIDE TIP: Rest stops can save your life. Pushing past the limits of your exhaustion can push you over the edge.

Get Your Vitamin "T"

It's a sorrowful state in the human condition when touching is somehow considered wrong. Of course, I understand inappropriate touch is not acceptable. What I mean is the simple act of making contact with each other perhaps with hugs or handshakes. Lately, any form of touching implies high risk for spreading infection or mounting a legal action. I even overheard a company CEO remark to staff that were in the midst of a greeting that shaking hands was a "no-no." As they quickly made a mid-course correction, rapidly withdrawing their outstretched hands, I heaved a sigh. The longing that results for all of those who feel like solitary units rather than interconnected beings of divine origin, is a painful reminder that we have somehow missed the boat on realizing our oneness. Anyway, I recall thinking about the way that we want to be loved and comforted, and the multitude of ways that we pursue those simple acts of kindness from those we love, often being misunderstood, ignored or rejected. Then the Black Cat taught me what no human being could; namely, that he needed pets and hugs like a nutrient that allowed him to sustain life. Vitamin "T" was a necessary part of his diet. It was right up there with canned tuna. There wasn't a day that went by when he didn't solicit a pet or hug. He made sure to get his daily allowance every single day of his life. Because of his teaching, I had gotten into the practice of not missing out on morning opportunities despite the mad rush to get out of the door. I started giving him 21 pets as he sat on my lap in the rocking chair and discovered that by meeting his need, I joyfully met my own need to enhance my connection to others. The Black Cat was a model of how to get people to pay attention to the need for touch, and we are all better for his example. The week after the Black Cat "passed on," I found myself seated in a posture in my yoga class thinking about the wonderful people in my class, and suddenly it came to me that at the close of the session, I would shake each person's hand. So as not to endanger or create concern, I cupped my two hands over the outside of their hands that I gently pressed into a prayer-like position. I extended my thanks to them and they received this simple gesture purely in the way that it was intended; smiling and nodding gestures of mutual gratitude. If you have a Vitamin "T" deficiency, do as the Black Cat and get it taken care of before another day passes.

> **ROADSIDE TIP: The primary purpose of taking the trip of life is to make connection. Don't overlook the opportunities to get in touch.**

Keep the Peace

The Black Cat's story began as a "tale of two kitties." He joined a household that already had a cat; an older female. The two were immediately locked in a tense relationship that was marked by the Black Cat's unwanted advances and troublesome pranks. Being the younger cat, he did the typical things like playing with the older cat's tail as though it were a bird in flight. He would pounce and move about quickly, sometimes startling the other cat or prompting a defensive frontal attack from her. Unlike the Black Cat, the older female cat was a martial arts master who, with remarkable speed, would launch an attack leaving the offending party with an array of scratches delivered with precision at lightning fast speed. Each had a technique for ignoring the other, and in no time at all they settled into a pattern of mutual disregard. It was never a blended relationship, but even that was a remarkable lesson. In retrospect, I appreciate the fact that peace is not always a matter of getting parties to coalesce, but to just co-exist. They preserved their primacy in the household and their innate integrity by agreeing to disagree about the rules of conduct and engagement, and carving out their own unique places in the world. Perhaps we could, likewise, learn that peace need not always be about the happy endings of complete union and synthesis of ideas, but of respectful acceptance of irreconcilable differences. Both cats lived their days in a world that acknowledged their uniqueness and the qualities of their inter-relationship; thereby, creating the kind of peace that suited the way that they shared their lives.

ROADSIDE TIPS: Share the road peacefully and recognize that your version of peace need not be compatible with others on the road. A genuine respect and a little forgiveness can be simply conveyed through calm indifference.

Whisper a Secret to a Friend

On the days when I was immobilized by illness or drawn into moments of quiet reflection upon my bed or sofa, I would quickly be joined by the Black Cat. He would land atop the bed or sofa and predictably start to paw the covers and cushions preparing to take his rightful place. When I joined him preparing for our rest, he would occasionally look over at me as if to ask, "What's the occasion?" This would initiate my ritual response of summoning his sacred trust, as I confessed my secret pain or suffering. He was never too busy to visit me or to accept my sorrowful state; therefore, it made me feel in some strange way that things would be alright, and the mood or the trouble would promptly pass. When you are sick and vulnerable, you crave the patience of a friend to steadfastly stay by you and help you through. The Black Cat was the same and treated me the same no matter if I was sick in bed or simply resting. He would sometimes perch right on my chest, looking me straight in the eye. His in and out breath created a roller coaster ride that slowed my breathing and calmed my troubled spirit. This made it easier to whisper a secret and slip quietly into the healing slumber of a cat nap.

ROADSIDE TIP: You don't have to travel alone over rough terrain. Take a trusted guide and let them help you navigate. Use your GPS (Good Personal Support).

Carry On

Early on, my daughter introduced the Black Cat to a way of being carried that he really seemed to enjoy. She would carry him like a baby over one shoulder, supported with an arm and a hand gently stoking his back. Sometimes he would struggle to get into that position and scratch you in the process. Once there, he would purr and sit contentedly looking about the room as if a tourist on an exciting excursion. I never discovered the true length of time that he could be carried thusly without stopping. It appeared that he could stay that way for hours, which meant that you would walk about from room to room showing him all there was to see. When I wanted to give him a special treat, I would put him on my shoulder and parade him around. As time passed, I did this less frequently. Then the practice came to mean that I would do it when I wanted to make amends for an oversight or an unintended slight, and would pick him up and show him around to make up for it. After a long absence due to traveling for business or pleasure, I would scoop him up and reward his patience with this customary walk. He always made me feel that no matter what, he could recover and I could feel reassured. If only we could all feel the same way as we experience the challenges and difficulties of life that make us want to retreat to a place or an activity that could help us carry on. The Black Cat never seemed to doubt his worthiness, and never shunned an opportunity to be carried about in his favorite way; likewise, he never doubted that he would "carry on."

ROADSIDE TIP: Be confident on the journey and know that you are capable.

Know When to Change the Litter Box

Life gives us lots of experiences. Some of them fill up pages in a diary or journal, while others are better suited to the litter box. And so it goes. We proceed on the journey of life busily acquiring an understanding of that which helps us grow: the food we eat; the amount of sleep we get; and the company we keep. We discover that there are other experiences that can make us feel that something was handled badly; or that certain people don't like us; or that we are on the losing side of life. We hold on to those bad experiences and when there is the slightest possibility that we will forget or move on, they are spontaneously resurrected and we are instantly thrust out of growth mode. Well, the Black Cat knew exactly where his food and water dishes were; where to get comfort and pets and how to keep himself well rested to grow healthy and strong. He also knew where to put the other experiences, so things would not get mixed up, and when the litter box was full he knew how to remind us to empty it. I pass the same advice on to you. Don't store up all the hurts and painful memories that happen to you. Hold on to the good stuff and know when to empty the litter box of all the rest.

ROADSIDE TIP: Bad stuff can build up clogging up the works and making you feel stuck or frustrated, so remember to change the oil just like you would clean a dirty litter box.

Ask for What You Want

The Black Cat was a talker. He would cry in ways that sounded like actual words. For example, in the morning he would say, "Now." At other times when he wanted my attention he would say, "Ma." In between, he could drive you to distraction with an endless chorus of "Meow." He would not tire of demanding what he wanted and usually, because of his persistence, he would get it. This is excellent advice for those of us who imagine that others can read our minds. They know what we want because of all of the clues we have given. They understand what we mean because it's "common sense." Our friends know why we are angry, and the subway traveler next to us surely knows that their music is both loud and disturbing. The message is an old one, but something tells me that even though the Black Cat understood it, many humans fail to comprehend that if you want something, you have to ask for it. If you aren't heard the first time, I'm certain that the Black Cat would recommend that you repeat it. It will take a stubborn indifference to the opinions of others that might make you want to stay silent, but with the boldness of the Black Cat, I urge you to make some noise.

ROADSIDE TIP: Sometimes your best companion and teacher on the trip is a pet. Pay attention and you will learn a great deal about unconditional love and how to ask and get what you want.

Chapter
15

FAILING GRACE

On the road of life winning can be a second place prize

I just returned from participating in a 5K run to "Help Fight Drug Abuse." I did it for a variety of reasons including an alignment with the cause, but perhaps more importantly because being alive gives you opportunities to try new things. This was a first for me and I guessed that there would be a meaningful lesson to go along with the souvenir T-shirt, so after much deliberation I settled my mind on a plan to participate that was unannounced to my family and friends. Next, I mulled over the important logistical details and on a promising Sunday morning, I got up at 5:00am and proceeded to warm up with my customary stretching. As I think back, the motivation for this decision came equally from a sense of commitment to the cause, an effort to seek meaning through contribution and a desire for personal growth.

I started out running and set mini-goals marked by parked cars along the side of the course. Each time I reached a goal, I would pledge to run just another car length. In between, I thought about removing the number and heading off down the block toward my car. Somehow I kept going and as I raced, I pondered many things including the hum and rattle of the police car that "brought up the rear." When I heard it I knew it meant that I was in the back; and as I went on, I initially tried to run from it to put some distance between us. Finally, I entered my groove as the very last person and felt a certain contentment with my position. This led me to a beautiful insight.

The police car slowly humming and rattling over the steamy asphalt on this very hot summer morning was Death and I said to myself, "As long as I keep moving, it won't overtake me," and we kept a respectful distance. I thought about my younger self as a faster, stronger, more agile runner full of summer and powered by cheap tennis shoes. I recalled the youthful me who would run without tiring, with no thought of an end; self-assured that no one could catch me. Certainly, Death was not even considered as a challenger. Now, in this race, I felt a strange comfort emerging and an ease with it just behind me. It's as if it was there to protect, hold and guide me on this winding part of my journey of Life. The more I ran, the more Death started to feel like the certainty of a place holder; a divine, kindly force that stayed with me when I wanted to veer off and retreat to my car. The police car continuously hummed and rattled up the incline, around the curve in the road, down the straightaway, around the bend at the end of the course where "angels" handed out water, praise, encouragement and patience to fuel the runners for the return trip.

I started back to the finish line and the car was still with me, merging in a way, determined as we both were to finish what we started. On this part of the race, I lost Ego that was running with me. Actually, I probably lost it at almost at the very beginning as I settled into the realization that I was dead last. What a fascinating experience. I have never desired to be last, but every race has a person who crosses the finish line last. I started to amuse myself with the thought that the first and last runners have most of the attention. The last runner plays a part that folks usually don't want, but I began to like it in a way that I never imagined I would. I started to take comfort from the car humming and rattling, ever to my back, churning out a tune of forgiveness for a presumed failure while I hummed a melody of satisfaction for the fulfillment of a personal challenge that started before my foot made the first step on the pavement. At each point, I challenged myself to go to the next step and felt victorious at each stage. I surprised myself at every milestone measured in car lengths and street corners. I would think, "I will run only to the end of this block," or "Maybe I will go a little farther …a little faster."

Finally, I crossed the finish line in fifty-two minutes facing a woman who cheered me on and a photographer who snapped a picture. I think that this experience has put a few things into perspective. I can be last and that can be a good place for me because I completed the race when my initial intention was to just give support with a donation. In the end, giving a donation and not running seemed like buying a plane ticket and not taking the trip. I met my perceptions of Death and was liberated from fear. I discovered that failure, like success, is only defined by your intentions. If I intended to win, I failed; but if I intended to finish, I succeeded. I experienced me unadorned by Ego and without my story of how I don't run. I created a new story should I choose to share as I am doing now, and I got a souvenir T-Shirt in the bargain.

ROADSIDE TIP: You never know how far you can travel until you strike out and get on the road; even if the destination is unfamiliar and the outcome is uncertain. Fear of death and failure are the roadblocks that can inhibit your progress or provide you with an opportunity to pass through them and come out on the other side.

Chapter
16

COME HOME

Sometimes we go in circles back to where we started

Much of what you have been looking for at the gym, in the therapist's office, in the shopping mall and in the beauty salon can be found right in your own home. Yes, I am surprised, too. I left home many years ago in search of self-esteem, society's appreciation, and a means of independent support for my needs and wants, and a photo ID that acknowledged that I existed because when I left homemakers weren't routinely given such things. After over thirty-five years in exile, I discovered that no one could have given me those things; instead I had to create them within myself, which I did. I went out there to trade with my bachelor's degree in hand, and I returned home now with a doctorate. I realize that no one gave it to me, I earned it and in order to earn it, I had to have a high regard for myself and my abilities. I had to withstand self-doubt, multiple competing demands and countless hours of work and deprivation. In the midst of the work toward that accomplishment, I nurtured my significant relationships with my husband and children, and even attracted some superb adult friendships which I found utterly surprising because I didn't think it was possible to have it all.

Women's liberation was a major catalyst for my believing that the home I felt trapped in had exits and suddenly the aprons, rolling pins and certain responsibilities slowly became relics of a half-remembered past. Those of you who recall this as I do will better understand my message, but the message is for us all. Perhaps it is a tale of discovery and I urge you to join the fun. Take the journey with me back home and discover the vast and numerous treasures that celebrate the womanly arts, exalt the feminine principle; and heal the wounded body and soul more effectively than any power lunch; boardroom victory; fabulous pair of shoes; six figure salary, or new workout. It is more than a mere pendulum swing to return to our true seat of power as a wise woman; visionary matriarch; intuitive healer; beacon of Light; spiritual teacher; green goddess; temple of grace; or keeper of the flame. It is a reclamation of worldly pursuits that are metaphors, symbols and vehicles for the goal of perfecting the soul.

The truth is that any action governed by spirit will yield powerful results, and there is a vast array of possibilities to pursue. Coming home frees women from the denial of the feminine nature that has been forced into a strange conformity largely shaped by the world of work outside the home. Coming home helps in the cultivation of harmony, balance, meaning, purpose, love and peace; as well as the promise of a fit mind, body and spirit. For those who have never left home, this journey will be an affirmation, and perhaps a revelation about the unexplored depths of the experience. For the young woman contemplating a direction, this journey may inform her choices and give her a new appreciation for home-based pleasures.

This return trip is as significant as the earlier departure because those who return understand the value of home; have a basis for comparison and a greater sense of proportion and perspective. Women need not be household drudges to fulfill this divine calling, or care more about the home and others than they do themselves, but by caring for themselves through the rites of keeping house, they are enhancing their capacity to care for others in the process. The world of work has taught us about beginnings and endings, so we have learned how to take breaks. We have learned that we are living longer than our turn of the century forbearers, so we need to take care of our bodies. We learned that taking a masculine approach to work and life has catapulted us to number one for stress related illnesses such as heart disease. We've learned that our labors are worth something, so we reward ourselves with appropriate compensation, and we recognize that a loving nature begins with loving ourselves and feeling worthy. So, come home and join me in re-experiencing the wonders of the womanly arts in full expression as we move through our homes and the activities of daily living and thriving.

Premenstrual Hammering and Menopausal Maintenance

Two things women are cautioned about are making noise and hitting things. We get a double blessing when we stumble upon an action that includes both. Just by chance while relishing a day out of the office, I tackled a project that lay dusty in my overloaded, overworked mind for months and months. The wobbly, bargain priced chest of drawers that was more glue than guts, wearily creaked and nearing total collapse, stood before me crying out for help. This particular morning I heard the cries more clearly even than the night before when in a gesture of support, I assembled wood glue and a hammer. All this, of course was alone worthy of my husband's attention and curiosity. Still, perhaps a night's slumber would with the 'morrow put said task back upon its resting place on the proverbial back burner. Please let me add that just the day before, I had been in the eleventh day of the winter blues and retreating into sleep to escape the pangs of boredom steeped in thick pools of drowned energy.

Well, the clock summoned me and I arose eager, dare I say enthusiastic, about my prepared list of tasks to perform. When my husband began stirring, I asked the whereabouts of the nails to which he inquired, "What are you going to do with those." Proudly, with hammer in hand I said, "I'm going to fix the cabinet." He fell silent, perhaps in disbelief because he generally repairs everything from computers to toasters, lighting to floorboards. Full of the determination of one approaching a personal Everest, I sorted through the nails which were as unique as any group of women. Some were thin and long; some short and thick; some with grooves and some that were smooth.

I grabbed a random assortment and headed for the living room where the "body" lay in state. As I approached, I imagined the chest of drawers whimpering at the thought of how it would be defiled by my reckless hands. A drawer that had totally come undone was resting on the top. Inside its four cornered essence was the glue and hammer duo. I picked up newspaper and covered the top of the cabinet as I lifted the collapsing drawer. My work was to begin. I glued the grooves that held the sides, then the corners and pressed each side together with its opposite. Walking away to attend to another chore, I would glance at it as I passed by on my busy way. I noticed that, as suspected, glue would not hold the parts securely enough. Now was the time for hammer and nails; the fateful moment when in the empty house, recently vacated by my husband who left for work, I stood free and unafraid wielding the hammer with my husband's instructions echoing in my head, "Hold the hammer at the end striking it directly, so that the nail won't bend." I did just that and the nail went right in, straight and sure. The next one bent and I yanked it out appreciating the self-correcting nature of my pursuit of excellence. The next nail popped across the floor and has not been seen. Then, as I found places to insert nails, I marveled at the wonderful noise that declared my triumph. I enjoyed the sound; the force of will and the meeting of my head and the head of the nail. I had done as the Tao instructs, overcome the duality of me and the nail realizing that the hammer and nails, glue and assorted parts had all been in celebration; joined in the unified field of infinite possibility.

If you are in the throes of a premenstrual fury; a mid-life crisis, the winter blues or a post-menopausal malaise, go get a hammer, maybe some glue, a board or stump and a bunch of nails. Walk out onto the field of battle confident and sure. Let the hammer give you a voice; let the glue hold you to the proper place and summon the nails to drive your message home. And as you stand there focused in the present moment, you will be set free.

ROADSIDE TIP: Make some noise and aim steadfast for your target or destination. Don't be taken off course even by your own self doubt.

Chapter
17

WHO WE ARE

Say My Name

Women are born in the river of change, and who they start out to be is altered by the winding current of life. I sit here wondering how to describe that stage of life when women have empty wombs, but full hearts and minds. I am talking about, the time of life when a woman stands upright in her truth and feels no discomfort. A woman in this stage of life sheds pretense and folly for the true reckoning of knowing that the shadow in daylight and her solid form are as different as she from her youthful self.

Curiously, she is also the woman who leafs through magazines looking for images displaying her glory; and when she can't find them, she puts her own head on a thin model and pictures herself in clothes that fit a waif.

She doesn't want to be called a "crone" and "mature woman" because they only conjure up the image of television advertisements for prescription medications and incontinence. "So who are we?" I ask, speaking as I must, as a member of this group.

I thought that every really important thing gets a name, so who are we? Women of a greater age; an older woman; these vague familiar references seem to describe someone who is annexed to a part of the imagination that is without words; banished by lack of definition;

yet, many can be seen riding the trains every day; catching a matinee or lunching with friends between trips abroad. Sometimes she is the well-dressed woman handling a banking transaction just a few feet away; or the one standing in the cold watching her grandchildren play. She may be the volunteer at the museum or hospital; or the one still putting in eight hour days in the workforce. But, who is she, really?

The woman in mid-life doesn't quite capture it because to be in the middle of something, you need to know the end as well as the beginning, and that is yet to be determined. I am uncomfortable because I thought it would be easy to capture this elusive creature in the paragraphs of my brief essay; however, I am undone.

As I surrender to my defeat, I will go for broke and tell you what I think without the use of a "catchall" phrase to describe this woman:

*She is **Radiance***, *not from the spotlight that shined on her in her youth, but from the inner reflection of a Spirit that makes her the lighthouse for her own journey on the sea of Life.*

*She is **Grace***, *with movements that slow the pace and deepen appreciation of the moment and each step on the path. Being careful not to fall, she relishes the gift of moving gracefully through her days.*

*She is **Confidence***, bursting forth like the place in the river where a vessel breaks into waves that crash on the shore.

*She is **Patience***, returning to stillness; listening in silence; waiting while others dash about searching for what ultimately can be found conveniently placed right at their feet.

She is Power, in her glance that delivers as much meaning as a volume of philosophical text.

She is Timeless and Monumental, in her capacity to recall her ability to consort with the Divine to transform reality from the smallest cell of hope into another being of Life.

She is Spirit, the substance of joy and sorrow that she elegantly wears as if they were made just for her expression.

She is Brave, beyond measure to be ever present in the face of an approaching end that can be seen in the distance.

I suppose that it is not surprising that we cannot name her because she was born in a river of change, and no sooner do we think we know her than she is transformed; and when we meet her on the road as it winds to its ending place, we need not call her by name, but simply nod because, after all, she knows who she is.

> **ROADSIDE TIP: Before you expect others to know who you are and call you by name, you must first know it.**

Chapter
18

THE PROMISE

A Tribal Tale of Reclamation

It is with great rejoicing that my people welcome each Spring. From the youngest to the oldest, they know that Spring is the bringer of new beginnings. The Earth's heart beats a slow refrain and with its every breath, the land swells with life. Storytellers whisper tales of the grapevine that appears dead in Winter, only to reawaken as the Earth warms. The women prepare to tend their gardens and the children sing their songs to the sun. And all wait in sacred anticipation as the time arrives.

Spring means that the rivers swell with sparkling water and the meadows blossom with life giving food. Spring means that the sky's lamp will stay upheld even longer each day, and the Earth will exchange seeds with a thankful people. As it approaches each year, I am reminded of these stories of my childhood and the sweet slumber of Winter that gives way to another Spring, summoning joy and love.

One day, a little girl asked her mother, "How does Spring know when to come, and how can we be sure that it will remember to come every year?"

It's a promise," her mother said. "It's a promise that has always been kept…but you are right, it is not something we can take for granted."

"What do you mean?" the little girl asked.

"Well, as I recall," the Mother continued, "each year Spring arrives because someone among us is asked to make a sacrifice without knowing why."

"What does that have to do with Spring coming, Mother? What about Spring?" the child insisted.

"For as long as I can remember, a man or woman has always consented to make a sacrifice so we all can have Spring," the Mother responded.

"Mother, how does someone know if they have been picked," the child asked.

"They don't," the Mother said, "it must be done without thought of getting something in return; without thought of the cost. They must simply be prepared to make the sacrifice when the time comes."

That year Spring's arrival was delayed. The cold winds chilled the branches as they reached higher and higher toward the sun. Rain did not fill the icy streams and rivers. The sky's lamp dimmed early.

The Earth's lips were drawn closed by the frigid cold of a lingering Winter, and she would not take or give seeds. The birds were waiting to sing; gathering together and flapping their wings in dismay. Every story told in the lodges ran on without end. No new beginnings came to break the Winter's tale.

The child went back to her mother and asked, "Mother, why is Spring taking so long?"

"I don't know, dear, but we must be patient. Remember, it's a promise," the Mother told her daughter.

As the days passed, the little girl began to doubt the truth of the promise.

"I don't think it will come, and I am tired of waiting," she said.

"It is easy to become discouraged," said her Mother, "but I have seen this happen many times...and Spring has always come. Even in the year of the great famine when your father died and there was no food to eat and little water to drink."

So the little girl waited; watching, wondering and hoping.

One night he sat upon her bed gazing out at the night sky filled with jeweled stars. A sudden pain overtook her tiny boy and she cried out to her Mother. When her Mother came in, she saw the girl enduring what was surely intense suffering. She summoned the healer to come immediately, but he could do nothing to loosen the grip of this mysterious affliction.

The mother said, "My child, my child...what is happening to you? What am I to do to help you?"

Without hesitation, the child replied, "Do nothing. I will bear this pain and it will last seven days. On the seventh day, Spring will come."

"How do you know this to be true?" the Mother pleaded.

"I simply feel that it is so," said the child.

The days passed slowly and the child drifted in and out of wakefulness as if on a raft in a troubled sea. The dawn of the seventh day was the same as every one before—cold, gray, lit only by a small lamp of light.

Awakening from a difficult night's slumber the Mother suddenly arose and walked across the floor to the place where her daughter slept. As she approached, she heard the sound of birdsongs growing louder with each step. When she looked at the bed, she saw the bedspread covered with flowers and warm sunshine beaming over it. Through the window she could see crystal waterfalls and blue sky.

The Mother frantically searched beneath the covers for her beloved child, but could not find her. After looking so long, she sat weary and sobbing on the bed. She wondered what she could have done to protect

145

her child. In her despair, her tears watered the coverlets and more flowers bloomed. She sobbed and the birdsongs filled the air.

In desperation, she pounded her chest and shook her fists saying, "Why did my child have to be sacrificed?"

As she turned and lifted her face to see through the open window at the bright sky, she saw her child's face; beautiful and free from pain and suffering.

"Why did you have to go?" the Mother asked.

"Because, Mother, Spring was not going to come this time," said the child.

"But how did you know? It has always come in the past...each year a man or woman was chosen. Why were you chosen?" she sobbed.

"Because no man or woman could be found. They all refused the sacrifice. They refused to sacrifice so that the world could have Spring," the child said.

On my dear girl, I will miss you so," her mother said as she lifted her head again toward the open window.

"You will only have to miss me in the months of cold. Remember me as you see me now, and I will return each year in the Spring to be with you," the child said. "Do not fear, do not worry... I am with you always."

And so it is. Each year Spring arrives; a promise from the Earth, and my people assemble to sing songs that praise the child who gave them Spring.

ROADSIDE TIP: Nature invites you to the open road. Be sure to show your appreciation by treading lightly and honoring the Earth's gifts with care and responsible concern; and celebrate the miracles that

unfold before you with gratitude and stewardship that demonstrates a personal regard for self and others.

Let this be your sacrifice to provide for future generations.

Chapter
19

PHOTO CLIPPINGS

Travel Photos

I f I were to tell the story of my life, I might be tempted to leave out some of the more challenging passages that, in fact, have created the uniqueness of my life; much like I cut the excess and unwanted portions off of photos that are too big for the album, or discard those that are too unflattering to be kept. Both actions create an inaccurate record, leaving out details that add fullness and truth to the cumulative account of my life. Each edits memories to fit rather than to recount realities that give significance, if not charm, to the episodes of weight gain; the deep depression captured in an empty stare; or red teary eyes as I dropped my child off for summer camp. Just as we omit the ugly pictures; cut and alter others, I create an idealized collection of memories tailored to match my denial and need for perfection.

Well, this is where I deposit a few of the clipped portions of my photos I so proudly exhibit. This is where I show the gallery of photos depicting some hard stares at Life that caused me to get knocked down.

The first insert in this album comes from the Spring of 2000 when I had lost sixteen pounds, developed shaking hands and a rapid heart rate to go with a metabolism in hyper-drive. Warnings appeared as early as March when I casually remarked to a co-worker that I felt as though my heart was racing. Two months later I dropped three dress sizes and fell into a pit of despair as I contemplated the possibility that I was not only ill, but severely depressed.

Something happened to me and I wasn't sure exactly what it was. If you're hit by a car, you know why your body is broken. If you experience a predictable life cycle event, you get another set of clues, but if you are well one day and suddenly find yourself dramatically changed the next, you start to worry. That worry quickly turns into fear and what you don't know or understand you manufacture into a variety of dire possibilities for what is plaguing you.

I thought about mental illness, menopause, but never thought my body was telling me something about the condition of my spirit or emotional life. So, I stayed in the dark, nursed my pain with an array of cures that even included a magnetic bracelet.

I pulled myself away from the urgent demands of work to take an overdue, brief two week holiday in Florida, hoping to restore what I had obviously lost. My response to all the things I generally love such as the warmth of the sun and beautiful, peaceful surroundings were the opposite of what I usually felt. I was too hot in the sun and too sad to enjoy the beautiful scenery. I managed not to melt down, but I felt so empty and alone. Finally, I concluded after much hesitation, "Something is wrong." This prompted me to engage in some self-examination that took me over the events of the previous few months. Suddenly, I could trace the chain of events that took apart my sense of health, well-being and peace of mind. Causes of illnesses are not always dramatic and understandable, or so I was starting to see.

I started off the New Year in January with money worries left over from the previous year. They were not even the type of money worries that rip out all or some of your supports. The matter was a small one. A consultant fee that was owed to me was seriously delayed. After repeatedly checking on it, I found that there was a problem. It turned out that someone intercepted the check, fraudulently signed my name and cashed it. I initially felt violated and later dishonored as the institution issuing the check put me through a grueling process to substantiate my innocence and establish that I was not a person possibly making a fraudulent claim to acquire a second check. This process included a meeting; an affidavit from me and a protracted three month wait for a check that was already three months overdue.

Next, I experienced some professional growing pains and despite a core belief that I was not interested in a particular advancement opportunity, I allowed myself to be coached by colleagues into applying for a vice president position in my organization. This process took my innocent dabbling into the realm of possibilities and slammed me head first into a rock hard, closed corporate door that I fancifully tried to open.

Well, as confidence in my financial acumen, and professional future were shaken, trouble was brewing on two other fronts. My daughter was coming of age and preparing for her departure from our family household. Because this happened over weeks and months with some jarring confrontations and her periodic absences; set against a backdrop of limited information, my anxiety went through the roof with the same velocity that my spirits began to plunge to the basement.

Next, my work demands, or perhaps my compulsion to prove myself, sent me into an intense workaholic state. The thing that seemed to be hurting me the most was the thing I couldn't let go of. It's like the insanity of holding onto a hot poker in your tender exposed hand. I let the pressures, disappointments, fears and demands take over and I began to crash.

The first signs came predictably from my all or nothing thinking. Either I devote all my energy to this pending project, or it will fail. Either I get a chance to advance, or I stay stuck. Either I am involved in my daughter's plans, or I suffer the feelings of total loss as she goes in the direction of her own life transition. Either I get all the money on the anticipated schedule, or I'm a terrible money manager with no hope of a future as a businesswoman or a responsible person.

I was this walking skeleton who would perhaps be considered getting fit, if not for the fact that my spirit and demeanor suggested a dull, sullen quality that betrayed my efforts to keep up a front. Inside it was as though a wrecking ball had knocked down everything. This demolition left the outer shell standing while I was hollow inside; heavy rubble falling within my inner depths.

Sleep was a series of brief ten minute rests. My heartbeat would awaken me and my hands would shake uncontrollably. Logic and Reason had no place in the picture. I clipped them and fashioned an album of me smiling at the annual women's conference that I coordinate each year. I humbly asked my daughter to help as she had done every year, and then nervously waited to see if she would come. A friend at the conference apparently wanted Logic and Reason to be in the group shot we took, so she asked me what was wrong, and urged me to see a doctor.

More out of desperation than anything else, I finally scheduled an appointment with my doctor. I wore a pair of jeans that visually captured for the doctor how much weight I had lost by how far they dropped below my waist. After a series of questions and routine procedures, he shared his best guess that I was suffering from the effects of a hyperactive thyroid. To confirm his suspicions, he advised me to submit to blood tests to check my levels of thyroid hormone. His diagnosis made me briefly joyful because it gave me a name and possible cause for what I was feeling. In his words, "Has some *funky* stuff been going on in your life?" My reply was a resounding, "Yes." Maybe this stuff wouldn't shake someone else, but the power and energy I gave to it launched a full frontal attack on my immune system in the form of Life moving through me at hyper speed; expelling it rapidly to get rid of it out of fear and perhaps disgust. I was controlling events using my negative fearful thoughts and my disordered thinking, creating my disordered metabolic process. Together these things robbed me of my peace of mind.

Well, you would think that this experience would teach me the power of my thoughts, but the understanding didn't thoroughly take. Even though I slowly recovered over a two year period from this bout with hyperthyroidism; examined the causal factors; took steps to mend my mind, body and spirit; and learned about the "agents" that helped to spread the dis-ease, in the Spring of 2003, I found myself starting a new album; trying to clip the harsh picture of a woman who is still in need of large doses of self-love and self-care to harmonize with a good natured tendency to be a closet perfectionist, overachiever and workaholic.

This album opens with the death of my mother in December 2001, followed two weeks later by the birth of my first grandchild born to my emancipated, married daughter. Then, I celebrated my 50th birthday three months later. Each shot shows me smiling and summoning the inner strength to rise to the occasion. There are no photos of my Tuesday evening crying sessions that helped me recognize and release the feelings that were not for public viewing.

Uncertainties about a direction for my life and my work became a backdrop for these familiar snapshots. Fears about getting to the next level in my life, being fully expressed, creative and happy were questions, not answers in my mind, and I felt restlessly standing still.

My 51st birthday arrived and all I knew was that I felt a surge of optimism and power in spite of a year of doubts, great performances and a feeling that I had lost the ability to relax and release stored up stress and residual pain. A week following my brilliant debut as a fifty one year old, I was stricken with a violent attack of sciatica on my right side. In utter shock, I proceeded to deny that a) this pain would last, b) that it would curtail my activities, and c) I couldn't control it. Well, I was in for a wild ride that you won't see captured in the photos of my vacation I took three weeks into this nightmare. You won't see it in the shots of Easter or Mothers Day, or the pictures of this year's women's conference. All you will see is the cane that was part of my dress code from that fateful day when pain visited my body home.

The messages started coming in from my Life; giving me flashbacks of my experiences. I started a new album that showed a wiser woman who learned to aggressively pursue self care as a remedy for the neglect of self that results from too much caring for and being concerned about others and matters of the external world. It showed a woman who had regained peace of mind. The newest album found me searching for harmony.

The pictures changed over a two to three year period as the self-care practices became another job in which I balanced my need for exercise, leisure, intimacy, privacy and solitude. My borders were constantly invaded and I would repeatedly utter, "not now," "no comment," and "no pictures, please." The more I would insist the more I would be overrun, so I concluded that I needed to flee in pursuit of more time at the gym, more days off, more time alone, more time with family, more time with my husband, more time to be creative and more time to nurture my business. The tiny pain in my back echoed in my hip, then down my leg. Then, one day I was forced to leave my aerobics class early because of a jarring pain that shot through my calf. Just a few days later, my right side felt as though it exploded from within and I was brought down. Curiously, being brought down by a respectable pain such as this did not generate my feelings of guilt and shame and I, consequently, did not feel the least bit depressed.

The night before this violent episode, I had prayed to God to help me to banish the nagging pains that always plagued my lower back and legs; and the following morning as I arose from my bed, my right leg from my hip to my foot was in excruciating pain of an intensity I had never before felt.

After numerous doctor appointments, tests, an MRI, and a second opinion, I decided to have the recommended surgery on my spine to correct the structural problem that put pressure on the nerves and precipitated numbness and weakness in my right foot.

As I sat one morning at 5:00 am, awakened by the feeling that I may actually finally be awake in my Life, I leafed through this recent picture album and discovered yet another revelation presented by the rarely photographed Life Challenge. In this shot, I imagined a cloud laced in silver, and suddenly I was able to see it clearly, as if for the first time.

Balance can ruin me if I'm the one doing all the balancing because the number of things to balance increases exponentially. They didn't tell me that when I listened to the experts who guided my exploration of the well-lived Life. I noticed that peace of mind and well-being were the themes of the first album, as I tried to align and coordinate the meaningful aspects of my preferred Life. I took on more, did more, but continued to balance and juggle even when my arms grew tired; my spirit weak and my mind weary. I complained about a lack of energy that became chronic and energy drains that became routine. Life might just as easily have jumped up and said, "Move in for my final close-up," but instead it said, "Can we talk—let me show you my best profile for this shot," and so, I got to see Life up close and personal. I was surprised to find that Life is not about perfection; in other words, it has enlarged pores, as well as the occasional pimple to go along with that distinguished chiseled nose and intelligent brow.

My lessons are these:

1. "Pride cometh before a fall"- Get your head out of the clouds long enough to notice the bump in the road, so you don't fall over it. Don't get too wrapped up in all the details that cause you to miss the obvious.

2. Self-Love—Self-care is no substitute for self love. Loving yourself means valuing and fully understanding that you are worthy and you don't have to qualify; it's a given. You don't have to doubt that you are good enough or work harder to convince others. Your sole responsibility is to be kind to yourself and simply do your best.

3. Take Time for Yourself—Do this, but not until it hurts. If going for a full body massage depletes your already limited

energy, it's not a benefit—forego it and rather than add something; take something away.

4. The Gym—The gym, like any other form of recreation or self-care is a choice, not an obligation. If it's an obligation, it becomes work.

5. Plug up your Energy Drains—Plug them up with "silly putty" by adding humor as you identify and treat what is sucking out your valuable life force.

6. Quick Self-Assessments—Do quick self assessments of your Life by looking at the condition of your purse or the weight of your key chain.

7. Too much clutter and too many keys can tell you a lot about what's happening with you.

8. Carrying & Lifting—Don't emulate ants lifting 100 times their body weight. There will be consequences for overstressing your body while stressing your mind and spirit. Things we carry become symbolic of responsibilities, burdens and demands. The more you carry around, the less likely you are to simply let go.

9. On the Run—Any activity that represents running away will become exhausting over time, no matter if it is going to the gym, shopping or some other diversion that takes you away from being still and examining your Life.

10. Take Time to be Self-Impressed—Be impressed with who you are and how you came to be. See yourself as you have developed over time and be open to the possibilities of your hopeful future.

11. Express your Creative Gifts—Don't betray yourself with false expressions of your creative gifts. Working and functioning well at work or in your family and community

are not substitutes for well expressed creative gifts that are a big part of your unique, full Life. Sing, dance, write, paint, explore!

ROADSIDE TIP: Keep a few of your ugly photos; and leave in a portion of the pictures that show your bad hair day, or your luxurious love handles to remind you that Life is not perfection; it is a picture album that should be a keepsake. And every keepsake, by nature, is a real treasure.

Chapter
20

THE SLOW BURN

Don't Become Combustible

S tories can sometimes give us a safe way to learn; therefore, I share my story in hopes that this cautionary tale will spare you the experience in favor of the lesson. I will share how I came to understand that there is great danger in what we resist; danger in 'driving with the *brakes* on,' and perhaps most dangerous by far is allowing resistance to render you into a combustible state.

Having learned many life lessons, often at a high cost to mind, body and spirit, I foolishly presumed that I knew better than to toy with the negative emotions that produce resistance and ultimately lead to depression. However, in a post-operative state, upon returning to a new job after a customary eight week medical leave, I found myself seriously compromised by a longing to remain sheltered and self-directed in the safety of my home. When the latter reality found no expression I, then, submitted to the cruel reality that I indeed was back at my desk in the midst of work life challenges and a learning curve that felt like an endless turn in the road. Rather than submit, I fought not to accept that this was what I must do. I plotted my eventual escape while toiling at the task of responding to what was being asked of me. Needless to say, I felt little joy and usually ended the day strained and drained. This is the pain I put myself through. So began the *slow burn*.

I noticed my actions and attitude toward my circumstances, but had little insight into how my resistance started to create friction; ever rubbing, grinding, and scraping. I began to look and feel different. My inner light became barely visible and in the darkness a cold, dry brittleness took over. My attention went to the places where I would see others who resembled my pain and I remained stuck.

One day as I arrived home after having escaped through a passage at the end of yet another day, I felt ravenous and weary. In a very uncharacteristic way, I dragged into the kitchen fully clothed in my work attire including a scarf that hung about my shoulders. I flipped on the stove to heat something while reaching into the cupboard then, in utter astonishment, I realized that my scarf had caught fire. The initial efforts to put out the flames suddenly changed to a panicked effort to mash the fire out against the back of a nearby chair; being too afraid to drop to the floor because I didn't want take any additional time responding to my crisis. When I arose from the chair and realized that the fire was still burning my clothes, I called out in desperation to my husband who was in a back room. I yelled, "I'm on fire." He ran to me down the hall where I stood tearing at my clothes. In an instant, he wet towels and threw them over me as my son emerged from his room; and I was saved.

I am here today to tell you that the friction and the slow burn of depression, resistance and long held negative emotions can rob you of far more than your joy; they can rob you of your self-protective instincts that alert you to danger and, consequently, bury your intention to be present in your life. They can make you feel like surrendering to the negative emotions by putting yourself on auto-pilot. Just as your parents may have told you not to play with matches, I'm telling you not to play with that slow burn—it can fire you up!

> ROADSIDE TIP: Don't mix gasoline and the sparks
> of a dangerously flammable mood.

Chapter
21

INSIDE PARENTING

You get what you pay for at the pump

Their sneakers are new and their clothes are stylish. That two year old is sporting a leather bomber jacket and cruising the boulevard in a state-of the-art stroller that screams its own price tag. The little one year old is wearing a halter top and a mini ruffle skirt as she is carried into the park to celebrate her first birthday. Music is pulsing out a tune of lost love and the kids are all gathered around as smoke and profanity fill the air. The little ones shout to be heard and the birthday girl is seated upon a motorized pink car that all the kids quickly start to fight over. Other children who are in the park stand by and watch, and slowly move in for some chips or a ride.

The scene changes to the busy pre-teens begging for some money to buy new sneakers, and when the request is denied both parent and child get into an argument. In the next apartment, a teen is watching an "R" rated movie that convincingly promotes the fun that is derived from sex and drugs while the parent falls asleep on the sofa. Across the hall another teen is sneaking out to go hang out with friends.

Soon they are "grown" and the parent wonders where the time went and where the food money in the cookie jar got to. One youngster doesn't ask for money because he has his own. In fact, he buys things for his parent and no one asks questions until one day when the officers show up and he is off to jail.

This is a short story and one that begs the question: What did we put inside? Regrettably, we look back over the past and see that we put everything into creating *trophy* kids that could impress the neighbors at a glance. Later, we want to make sure they have everything we didn't have, so we put the finest sneakers on their feet while leaving their head uncovered.

Before long the bill comes due and we realize that we put everything on the outside and nothing on the inside. But wait, there is still time. Take out your pen and paper and write down your answers to this simple question: How would you feel and act if your were valued; listened to; protected; treated with care and held in high regard; trusted; believed. Next, write down how you would feel and act if you were disregarded; overindulged; treated badly; unprotected; distrusted and disbelieved. In your heart, you probably know the good stuff from the stuff that's not so good. And you suspect that Time will be on your side if you use it to watch and listen as the little one grows; making regular deposits of love and care that show them that what's inside them is all good *stuff* that will last longer than any toy or pair of sneakers.

ROADSIDE TIP: When it comes to raising kids, it's a lot like taking care of your automobile... for maximum benefit, make sure you put the best inside.

Chapter
22

AROUND THE POETRY CORNER

There's poetry around every corner of the journey

Poetry can help us to heal. Poetry gives a great sense of relief by freeing thoughts. Poetry has often been my salvation and my redeemer. It has amused me and brought me to tears. It has been a path to greater understanding at times of confusion and chaos. It has connected me to the larger shared vision that I hold in common with others traveling the same roads. My words have been like my children and I have watched them grow in their meaningfulness to my life as I have transitioned through years of change. There are three (3) basic categories of poems that I am sharing:

Nature has often been my inspiration and safe haven sheltering me as I looked inside. It has been with me when I was a lonely traveler and when I was a joyous seeker.

Love is another source of great inspiration for all on the road of life and I make ample use of this subject to propel myself along.

Survival has often prompted me into surrender and at other times, inspired me to greater self determination.

I offer these poems as some of the best traveling directions I have had on my journey.

Sharon M. Cadiz, Ed.D.

NATURE:

My Mother's Garden

It all grew there
On the trellis,
On the vine,
On the ground,
In the shade.

She gave me bouquets
That would be mine
To help me with a lifetime of sorrow and joy.

I bring them out to play
On the sunless days;
And when Spring visits my mind.

Thank you Mama
For the flowers of my youth.

Let Me Be a Robin

Let me be a robin;
Proud and quick.
Let me be its song;
Before the summer's harvest is picked.
Let me be the color that calls attention to the place.
Where the Creator made summer
And adorned it with a robin's grace.

Summer is My Cradle

Summer is my cradle
And return to it I must.
The circle of the seasons abide in my great trust
That summer will arrive again
And rock me gently in her arms
Reminding me of how she loved me
As a mere babe in arms.

One Day

One day I'll be a gardener,
But for now you are my garden.
One day I'll be a writer,
But for now you are my story.
One day I'll be a singer,
But for now, you are my song.
One day I'll be a river to carry life along.
One day I'll be forever.
One day soon I'll be gone.

When the Light Passes

When the light passes from my eyes
And the evening robin fades from view,
I will rest among the summer breeze and
awaken in the morning dew.

Fall, Again

Fall is the bittersweet remembrance of
The passage of time.
Enjoy it and be warmed by comforting memories.
Honor the falling leaves
As a tribute to our brave surrender of
Summer's hold on our hearts,
And be still as you breathe the cool stirring air.

Watching the Birth of Morning

Watching the birth of morning
I gaze out of my window.
I hear the early garbage runs
That summon the new day.
I smell the fresh unused air
As it waifs through my window.
I pause in admiration of the creative force of Nature
That fashions a new day
Out of what was left
From the day before.

Sharon M. Cadiz, Ed.D.

Ocean

The Ocean is a washer woman
Beating her clothes against the rocky shore.
The sudsy foam gathers and disappears
'Til the next thrust of of her powerful hands.
A silken garment of fine design unfurls;
Curled edge sheerness
Flowing down upon the surface.
Then it's twisted under the weight of her mighty arms
With fierce power and gentle energy.
Exquisite blues and greens; seaweed and shells;
Decorative assortment; tempting array.

Zen Fishing

Blessed refuge in the city,
Heartbeat from the ache of doom,
Tucked within this tiny forest
Within the city a tiny room.
I send my line into the lake,
Waiting for the gifts to take:
Wind sent ripples,
Ducks and geese,
Sun washed surface,
Relaxed bare feet,
Hungry fishes with peace to keep;
The rock lined shore;
The birds at work.
Zen fishing—
No worms, no dirt.

Faith is the Fisherman

Faith is the fisherman,
Standing hip high in water.
Creeping stillness sends peace through his soul.
He tosses his line to catch a dream;
The reward for a life of humble service.
He sees a fish frolic past his hook and fancies
himself the luckiest of men to know
The dream is real.
The glorious gift exists
Just beyond his reach,
Ever in his mind's grasp.
What happens when the fish
Stumbles upon the line,
Hooked by his desperate wish…
His dream come true?
He throws it back,
Satisfied with the compliment.

I Was Born in Many Places

I was born in many places;
Under a fig tree in Italy,
On the red clay of Georgia,
And in the sun of day
In the river that spoke me into life,
By a wigwam
In the village where African rhythms play.
I was born in many places
To be reborn anew each day.

Cut Flowers

Cut flowers thirst for more.
They fear the end at their very core.
The drying petals;
Bending stems,
Long to connect
To the Great Mother's limbs.
Drawing them closer,
Her promise to feel.
At the base of her roots
There to kneel
The Great Mother surrounds them
In a womb of love;
A cord of connection from the depths to above.

Cut flowers aren't lost, nor shall they perish;
They will find their way home without any peril.
They breathe in the air—
They take in the sun—
They revel in passions and frolic in fun.
They quiet themselves
Drawing their energy close
Vibrating and channeling what is desired most,
Then sending the intention down through vital stems;
Forming the roots at the very ends
The roots reaching blindly searching the depths;
Guided and supported with each conscious breath.
The roots are expanding in all directions and finally
     reach the Great Mother connection.

Cut flowers no more without destination—
Cut flowers no more without consolation—
Cut flowers no more in fear of isolation—
Cut flowers no more,
No more awaiting extinction.
Taking nourishment without fear
Standing tall standing clear.
I am the flower.
I am the root.
I am connected.
I am safe, secure peaceful, joyful and new.

Love

Mama
Mama hums when walking
There's music in her head.
Vibrations of a love force;
Poetry unsaid.

Kneeling at the Grave

I knelt at the grave to light the incense.
I knew that I had struck the match, but could not see the flame
In the light of day.
Suddenly, in the shifting light the orange flame appeared.
Such is the Spirit of my father and mother;
Invisible, but present.
In a certain light of slumber or a passing thought
I can see them.

Beyond Reason

When someone loves you
No holds barred
Unconditionally without a lapse
In the face of glaring gaps;
Loves you now and loves you later
There can be no greater favor.
Blessed are the ones who know
What Nature made can only grow
When Love is the soil and Acceptance the shower
When all that you do becomes a great tower
Withstanding hurt
Withstanding pain
Only to crumble and be built again—
So is the Love of all simple creatures
Who Love from a heart
Beyond all seeming evidence of Reason.

Think of You

When my thoughts are mine
I think of you
When I decorate my mood with fragrant mist
Amid the vapors you are heaven sent.

Between Us

We gave joy a shining moment,
Gave bliss a light decree.
For every desire spoken
A remembrance for me.

On a Feeling

Parting glances
Held in memory
Pressed upon the fragrant flower you gave to me.
Indelible portrait of what could be.

Time Spaces in Dreams

Inside my thoughts there is no time
Only a limitless plain
Only unfettered flight
Sun-filled days
Moonlit nights.

Scented Moments
Present tense
Parted lips
Whispers sent
On a gentle feeling,
In a warming smile,
Love-dipped moments
Coaxed to stay awhile.

Love Letters on the Wall

He writes his passion on the walls
Expressed in the intricate detail of orchid borders against
periwinkle;
And he etches a sonnet of love in the trimming that only he and I
notice—
The secret held between lovers.
And I sit at 3:40am at the table with warming tea and seal my
thanks in this verse.

Survival

An Umbrella Doesn't Always Keep the Rain Off
You gave it to me for cover in the storm;
Another layer of protection and warmth,
But it rains in torrents just inside
And despite my efforts, I can't hide.
The umbrella turns inside out;
The winds whir, whip and shout,
And I can't get the simple, desperate words out
Telling you although you mean so well
This umbrella can go to hell.
Teach me to stand the rain.
Help me to understand the pain.
Put me on a safety track.
Show me how to strengthen my back.
And I will, then, decide which day
To take an umbrella or let it stay.

Invocation

Pain gives birth to poetry,
Open faced or wounded—
A joyous birth or a sour ferment;
The prayer of a soul unbent.
Lift the eyes,
Dry the tears,
Open the heart,
Quiet the fears.
Bring me back to poetry.
Bring my words to light.
Stop incessant chattering
And still the pen to write.
Write of all the wisdom,
Hours of sadness spent,
Wishes and the like;
A stubborn will unbent.

Making Peace

There will always be unmade beds,
Unfinished tasks,
Disappointing falls,
Aggravating calls,
Unmatched socks,
Unwound clocks.
So among these things,
I must make my own special flings;
Times to laugh,
Times to fly,
Times to fittingly hug and cry.
I must myself be content to know,
As they came, so they will surely go.

Unaccompanied

I will paint my lips with pink,
Wear a dress of greater length,
Don dark socks
And a sweater wear;
Put a flower in my hair.
I will walk with tote in hand.
I will feel wholly grand
In spectator shoes
And shaded specs
I will redress a mood's manifest.

No Comment

"How are you today?"
I'm choking on my spit.
My clothes don't fit.
I feel like I'm in a dead end life;
Trapped as though by a terrorist with a knife.
There are no back doors,
Only ceilings and floors
And they're pressing in
So I can't win.
I'm caught and need company—
This would mean something to me;
However, my life just can't break out of cement,
So my reply is: *"No comment."*

Rhythm

I dance for myself and my feet have wings;
My soul opens up and the world sings,
But in the company of others
I'm stiff and still
They took my dance against my will
As I looked on and felt my arms grow too long.
My feet too big and my steps all wrong.
I cry today in memory of
The dance that was my own true love.

Pregnant in Purple
(View from the Project Window)

Purple leather coat,
Purple pants and blouse,
Plump mother of a premature prime.
Road warrior of the mean streets
Lost among the unwashed sheets;
Casualty of a misbegotten joke
Told to all young girls who don't know;
The whine and coo that summons their pear-shaped love
Transforming her to a pigeon from a dove.
Awestruck virgin of the emphatic conception
Feeling far beyond correction.
Staring blankly at the afternoon rain;
Calling for the key to get in out of her pain;
Knowing that none of the keys really fit.
I laugh, but its not funny to see you there
Without a clue.
Whoever knew the rules of Nature would suddenly apply to you.
Pretty in purple
She will not be,
No cloth or cape to cover the seed
That grows and changes her playdough world
Lost among the under grass, mysteries unfurled.

Sharon M. Cadiz, Ed.D.

Little Sister

Little sister smiles when she should cry,
Walks when she should fly;
Lingers as she tries to die.

Who Me?

Sometimes I think about the systematic dismemberment of
women
Reinforcing the idea that once you start to age
(I believe that occurs at birth)
You start to lose chunks of yourself.
They are small chunks at first,
And then get progressively larger.
In puberty we sometimes lose our virginity;
In mid-life we often lose our uterus.
Too often we lose a breast, an ovary, etc.
Well, I'm tired of these rules and assumptions.
I've given away the last chunk I plan to give away.
If anything leaves me, it will have to be taken by force.
I am the gatekeeper and nothing shall pass!

Carry Your Sorrow in Baskets

I carried Sorrow in baskets
Until it grew too large,
Then I found a barrel, but it was too hard.
I went to get a casket and I saw the wrong,
Not because it's scary, just too long.
Then I stopped and pondered
Why sorrow has so grown;
And I paused further, not seeking just to moan.
And later as I pondered,
I grew still at heart
While thinking perhaps a basket could carry every part.
Not just any basket;
Not just any kind.
So, off I went in haste,
A special one to find.
Now I have the basket;
The one to hold my Sorrow in;
A special *woman* basket,
No bigger than a pin.

PART THREE

ROADSIDE SERVICE

Chapter
23

WHAT TO DO WHEN
YOU GET LOST

Roadwork and detours can get you lost

This section is about what to do when you get lost on the journey of healing and recovery; seeking answers to why a particular detour led you down a wrong road. Handling speed bumps, taking detours and finding the way back to the main road is a challenge for most of us, but there are helpful ways to manage this experience because there are lessons that have been learned which can be shared and mastered. Feel free to use this part to redeem the roundtrip ticket and lifetime guarantee that you were given with your traveling shoes. Here are some snapshots from my travels that capture the different "views," that can be seen along the way.

Safe Space:
Define and describe your safe space. Use as much symbolism and detail as you like. Here is how I captured it:

The Beach

The beach is a metaphor for how I see and feel absolute unity. It is the place of beginnings and endings; expansion and recession; coming and going; giving and receiving; bringing and taking; being and manifesting; death and birth. I feel like a creature of both the sea and the shore. I have learned to walk on land and I have vague memories of swimming in the depths of the wide ocean. When I arrive, the sea birds chatter among themselves and gleefully welcome me back. Some come up to me to see what's new. I welcome their interest and feel like one of the family.

I walk from the concrete to the sandy dunes over and across until I reach my ideal space. The lifeguards are my protectors and as such, they are honored with a lofty throne. We all sit under the warming glow of a loving sun. The sun kisses my arms up and down like so many other times before, greeting me with a consuming bliss that engulfs my spirit. The sun praises me for rejoining the spectacle of nature's celebration. We are old friends and we share a dance.

The sand reaches up and grabs my feet to remind me that it is there to help me shed the callous grip of mundane pursuits that both wear me down and produce thickened armor. The false protection of calloused armor on my feet needs to be shed, so that I can feel the sun's gaze more fully; feel the sand's moist kiss; see the foaming excitement of the ocean; and the contrasting changes of the sky.

I sit to rest; just to be and drink in the scene of joyous homecoming. I unlock the tense muscles and rigid thoughts that keep me feeling locked in a box. I breathe in through the top of my head, taking in pure air and light that filters through channels of my body to reach all the vital areas unlocking; allowing; giving and receiving from every cell, muscle, joint and organ of a thankful body. I visualize myself and summon all good that is mine by divine right.

I contemplate all the messages from a loving body that communicates in a variety of ways: a twitch; tingle; ache all signals that tells me something I need to know. I am grateful to my body for speaking up and for helping me to keep a sense of balance created through proper self-care and active listening.

The beach is a safe, sacred space where I feel free. I am filled with joy and gratitude as I release the burdens that make life heavy—the past; worries; self-doubt; and feelings of want. Each morning, and at times during the day, I will return, summoning bliss.

Symbols and Meanings

*I fashioned a healing narrative that utilizes the following symbols describing how I often feel when I am overwhelmed. In meditation, I visualized myself in a variety of places including my safe space, in a lighthouse with a search light that represented my eyes; and as a shepherd tending a flock and caring for the land. In another meditation, a gold ring appeared to me. In each session, I was seeking relief from the anxiety and fatigue that manifested as pain and discomfort in the body. I saw myself consumed with the demands and needs of others and I sorted out what was beneficial and harmful by describing the aspects of my busy life as weeds or seeds. These things helped me to access the deeper aspects of what was the cause of pain and discomfort in my body. You can try to do the same thing in a state of deep inner reflection that scans the body and makes associations with symbolic meanings. I had a wonderful guide by the name of Kiana Love of **Be Wild Woman** who helped me with these efforts. She reminded me to breathe and to go to the area of pain in my body and explore its qualities (what it looked like; felt like; the color, and so on). By relaxing and scanning the body in this way, I achieve a greater state of calm and relief from the pain. You can try it to see if it could work for you. I offer you my own example of how this worked for me in the following details:*

The Meanings Attached to My Visualizations

Safe Space is the **Beach**

Sacred Space in the body: *Heart & Pelvic Area; anywhere I am*

Golden Ring *symbolizes* **Life;** *enlarges and is placed in the pelvic region marking the sacred space. Golden ring grows brighter with every deep, relaxing breath.*

Golden arc of branches and vines *at my feet is* **Protection** */comes up out of the ground*

Counsel *is a guiding force made up of peaceful, positive, guardian souls.*

<u>**A Necklace of two knotted colored strings and what they mean**</u> <u>**(choose your meaning for these colors)**</u>:

> **Red**: *Needs,-safety, security, support, freedom, abundance*

> **White**: *Intentions-safety, peace, illuminated bliss, gratitude, faith, prosperity, wisdom*

> **Knots** *symbolize* **Unity**

Weeds *are negative people or experiences*

Seeds *are positive intentions and growth experiences*

Cutting Off Connection *means "unplugging" or detaching from the needs and wants of others (in the evening). Giving permission to unplug*

Lighthouse *represents hyper vigilance and caretaking of others; always on*

Shepherd *describes how I get others to safety; protect and guide until I am sometimes depleted; frustrated; confused about how to relieve the suffering that seems to intensify-harder to relieve the pain; feeling that I need to do more/trying to let go of the consuming aspects of this role that usually leads me to feeling drained and neglectful of my own needs*

Eyes *need rest from seeing so much pain in the world*

Container of Care *means becoming a vessel of self-care for myself*

Pearl is a symbol of purity and healing—*it floats suspended in front of my spine; centered and sometimes spinning-internal view as I examine the pain in the muscles to either side of my spine*

Slow down and breathe- *relaxed, mindful breathing opens the doorway to the inner exploration*

Take in sensory information-*use the senses to describe where the pain and discomfort is in the body.*

Be curious and inquisitive-*explore in a relaxed manner with closed eyes in a resting position.*

Make a pledge that acknowledges a new, positive intention for your life's journey: (Here is an example of what I came up with):

Pledge

I will honor myself with the knowledge that I am enough. I have enough. I create my own container of care. I am safe, secure, supported. I reject being the container for the pain of others and the world, and serve best through my own healing, safety, peace and divine presence.

Words for the Journey

Harvest
Heal
Allow
Accept
Receive
Believe
Root
Release
Golden
Honor
Embrace
Roots
Nourishment
Faith
Support
Security
Freedom
Divine
Moon
Sun
Sacred
Meaning
Love
Curious
Inquisitive
Respect
Feminine
Energy
Cradle
Ease

Complete

Clarify

Power

Connect

Celebrate

Serenity

Surrender

Wisdom

Prosperity

Self-Care

Safety

New

Divine Order

Space

Value

Light

Senses

Sensory

Breathing

In:	Out:
Safety	Worry
Security	Fear
Support	Burdens
Simplicity	Chaos/Confusion
Strength	Fatigue/Weakness

Let these activities bring you back to your balanced self.

Chapter
24

TALK TO ME

Take an active role in your healing

One of the first things given to me as I was admitted to the hospital; before the slippers, gown and identification bracelet, was the word "PAIN." The youthful anesthesiologist, gave it to me in the admitting office while reviewing some forms and procedures. After he finished his presentation, I innocently asked, *"What can I expect the day after the surgery?"* He calmly replied, *"PAIN."*

It was this hard thing shaped like a rectangle with sharp corners spelling out P-A-I-N. I spent the night before surgery with it beside me in my lonely hospital room, trying to understand what it would mean to me the following day.

Well, the next morning at 6:45 a.m. a man in white who repeatedly said, *"I'm late,"* whisked me through the corridors to the pre-operation room where there was an impressive gathering of doctors in my honor. PAIN was still this rectangular word that lay beside me on the bed.

Within moments, the "IV" was inserted and I went away. When I got back, I found that they had removed something from me and put that hard rectangular word inside me (covering it over with a wide white bandage). It was stiff, heavy and unyielding. I squirmed to escape its horrible sensation; yet, I could not.

The nurse said that I could get nothing to chase the PAIN until the one unit of blood I had donated weeks before entered my body. So, I waited as my body contracted in a pressurized pain of abdomen, legs and lower back. Somehow, despite my lack of preparation for having PAIN reside so close to the marrow of my being, I survived two hours with it while watching the blood re-enter my body.

Next, I got my own PAIN chasing machine with morphine to end the oppression of PAIN's violent rule. My body seemed hardly to notice the difference between PAIN with chaser, and PAIN without, but I had the faith because they told me that relief coursed through my veins; banishing PAIN's echoing cries. I was even given the option of pressing a button to increase the PAIN chaser when necessary; and was assured that I couldn't possibly take too much. Well, I exercised my right with discretion and asked to be taken off on the third day although "PAIN" remained; weakened, but still there.

With each passing day "PAIN" grew weaker and moved closer to the "EXIT." At that point, I looked forward to handing it back to the doctor and saying, *"Here it is, you can take it back, now. When you give it to the next patient, I hope that person will manage it well and go home healthy and whole.* That is my wish for you. Manage your pain and become a partner in your healing and recovery.

I would like to use this portion of the handbook to support those who may be facing the experience of being hospitalized. I am astounded at the number of people who get out of the hospital alive; not because of malpractice or complications, but because fear and pain plague so many. I am simply amazed that patients succeed as often as they do in mustering whatever spiritual or physical strength it requires to emerge from hospitals. Perhaps the lucky ones need to share their secrets. I, for one, am willing to start.

Well, to begin, this section's title came to me as I reminisced over my numerous encounters with doctors who would not talk to me. Some talked at me, around me, but rarely to me. An obvious sequel would be "Listen to Me." The key ideas are: make choices, plan, prepare, fearlessly ask for what you want and need; and strive to be healthy, happy and whole. Although the reasons that lead to hospitalizations vary, I will briefly share some common experiences that patients encounter.

When you suspect a health related problem, make every effort to get comprehensive medical attention. There are often emotional hurdles threaten obstruct the way to medical care including such road blocks as denial.

Questions to Ask Yourself:

1. Will my condition worsen if I wait?
2. Will early treatment benefit me?
3. Are there sound reasons to wait? If so, what are they?

Even when you go boldly forth in pursuit of medical care, you may not be fully prepared for the physician's findings.

Questions to Ask Yourself:

1. Am I prepared for what the physician may say regarding my condition?
2. How can I prepare myself?

3. Where will I be able to turn if I need support, guidance, or more information?

Sometimes one can go for a routine examination and discover a problem that was not previously identified. Depending on the seriousness, you will need to chart a course of action t respond.

Questions to Ask the Physician:

1. Can I make and appointment for a consultation to review the details regarding the medical findings?
2. Give yourself the time needed to formulate your list of questions beginning with

    How serious is it?

    What are the treatment options?

    What is your recommendation? Why?

    What are the risks/dangers/consequences?

Following a thorough review and analysis of the situation, formulate a <u>Thre Step Action Plan</u>. Most solutions can be looked at simply and concisely in three steps.

Steps to Take:

1. _____
2. _____
3. _____

These steps can also be thought of as <u>GOALS</u>. To support you in this process, think of affirming statements, words, or phrases that draw on positive energy to propel you toward your goals:

Sample: *"This above all, to thine ownself be true..."* Shakespeare's <u>Hamlet</u>

Write or select three (3) of your own:

1. _____
2. _____
3. _____

Create your own vision of wholeness, looking at yourself at all times as a whole integrated being. To help you describe all of your roles, think about listing the title, roles and responsibilities you have. Take this vision into account when you begin to plan next steps.

Questions to Ask Yourself:

1. What areas of my life trouble me the most in relation to my condition?
2. What are my areas of strength? Weakness?
3. How can I strengthen and support myself?
4. How can I mobilize/activate friends or family to help and support?

Remember:
Get all the <u>facts</u>.

Take responsible <u>action.</u>

Be aware of your <u>assets.</u>

Bolster your <u>self-support.</u>

Identify <u>other supports</u>. (family, friends, networks)

Think <u>holistic.</u>

NOTE: *If you attempt to handle a health related condition or impending procedure without bringing order and clarity to your inner thoughts, you risk placing yourself at greater risk for complicating your healing and recovery process. You may even sabotage your efforts.*

ROADSIDE TIPS: You can often give your own blood, if a blood transfusion is a possibility or a certainty. This can usually be arranged two weeks before the procedure. Ask your physician about this and read the patient handbook. Consider taking a friend or family member to your appointments and especially to the Emergency Room. Arrange to be shown the hospital before you are admitted. Learn as much as possible about the physician's credentials prior to the procedure or hospital admission. Find out if the hospital has a patient advocate who can assist you if you have any complaints or concerns. Keep a log of all the physicians who examine you and the medications, tests and treatments you receive and check your list against your bill. Make sure everyone in the hospital knows who you are to avoid errors resulting from identity confusion. Write your selected surgeon's name on the consent form to prevent other physicians from performing your surgery or other procedure. Try not to be admitted on a Friday because you could spend the weekend waiting for laboratory test results. Take advantage of the option to select your meal menus.

NOTE: Check out the *People's Medical Society* for more information.

This section of the handbook is organized to be a help during a time when the emotions of fear and worry threaten your sense of stability, confidence and wholeness. It is designed in *inform* and *educate women* for positive health outcomes. Use it as a tool to promote healing through *awareness* and *action*. Take from these pages what you find helpful to the process, and add those things that enhance your individual experience of reclamation and empowerment.

As an aware partner working with your medical service providers, you will cooperate with the levels of healing that touch your *mind, body* and *spirit*. You will feel strong and fearless; not weak and helpless.

Have you ever gone to a medical appointment and tried to communicate with your doctor only to find yourself feeling like Charlie McCarthy sitting on Edgar Bergen's lap? It's as if there's someone else in the room who is regarded as having more knowledge than you about your body. Have you felt like shouting, "Talk to *me*! You only *think* I'm a dummy with someone else making the lips move."

So, having had this feeling more times than I can count, or care to remember, and because I have needed to communicate it to improve my chances for survival in this world, I presumed others might need to be supported in doing likewise. This is intended as a testament to what we can accomplish when we give ourselves a role in our own healing.

Even when you take your car for repair, the mechanic asks you what's wrong. Somehow, we are not regarded as the best authorities on our bodies when we take ourselves in for 'repair' or 'maintenance check-ups.' Years of experience with medical doctors convinces me both that too many are essentially mechanics, and further that many are not even good ones because they don't ask what's wrong, with the expectation that you will *really* have anything to add to their picture.

Well, like a mechanic, the doctor enters into a contract to fix what's broken and the very best doctors will do that flawlessly and you will be engaged, repaired and ready to complete your journey. However, in far too many cases a person's faith can be misplaced and they emerge from the experience with a new set of wounds.

ROADSIDE TIP: Monitor all the work that is done.

PART FOUR

PREVENTIVE MAINTENANCE

Chapter
25

SAFE ARRIVAL

Easy Does It as You Simplify, Modify, Gratify

In twenty years of producing seminars and conducting annual conferences on personal development, self healing and wellness, I have discovered quite a few life lessons that I would like to offer to help propel you toward greater heights of self expression healing, recovery and wellness. The insights have been drawn from my own personal journey of discovery and the shared experiences of hundreds of men and women who have marshaled the courage to take the trip.

Many of us feel grounded and stuck without a "flight plan" to get us to the next level. This section will help you get "lift-off" using some simple guidelines, stories and ideas. Most times we maybe traveling on foot, but when you, your plans, goals or dreams need to "take off,: you will probably need the special guidance that this section will provide.

Remember, you are always in first class; you have an open roundtrip ticket to fly solo or with a partner, and you are advised to check your unwanted baggage before beginning your trip. Carry on bags should contain your skills, talents, strengths, dreams, aspirations and aims; along with positivity, fearlessness, vision, creativity, non-judgment and non-resistance. The only thing that can send you crashing to the ground is negative thinking. If the self contained cabin is penetrated by unwanted negative thoughts or emotions, you will immediately lose altitude, and are advised to take three deep breaths; one each for the *mind*, *body* and *spirit*. Now, step aboard and enjoy the following "Rules for Take-Off.

Life's a Trip: Go First Class

Life is an interesting combination of events and beliefs that determine if we'll go through life in "coach" or "first class." Expectations are formed over years, and we buy into a notion of what we determine is our destiny. All too often we lock ourselves into a pattern of belief that rigidly defines who we are, what we need or deserve and how successful we will be. The truth is, despite birth circumstances, we were all assigned to first class with unlimited access to abundance, prosperity and fulfillment. Somewhere along the journey we began doubting the truth of this, presuming that abundance is wealth and prosperity is fortune, and fulfillment is achievement.

This belief that some are destined to prosper and others are not is an untruth that forms class bias, promotes low self-esteem and even racial conflict. Curiously, however, if we go back and start with the truth, all of these things seem absurd. Going back to the truth is itself a challenging journey for which we can prepare. We must train ourselves to recognize how we sabotage our pursuit of the truth.

For example, some people never leave the airport; never quite take-off. These are the folks who are compulsively "getting ready." They need the right everything/they need to wait until they retire, or the kids grow up, or they need to complete some more courses, get another degree. They will say that they don't have the right luggage, or enough money. They may even insist that until all their conditions for a *perfect* trip are met, they can't go. They spend their lives "getting ready." They let a sudden illness of a family member; the setback of a friend, or their own personal problem de-rail a plan to "take-off;" to cash in their ticket for a first class life. They stumble around exhausted shopping for designer glasses and Coppertone, and ultimately miss the plane. It's not necessarily settling for less to entertain the possibility that the exotic adventures of a first class life can be just as easily enjoyed with a dollar pair of sunglasses in an Armani case.

Rule #1: You are always in first class with an open ticket to fly as often, far and wide as your dreams and imagination can dictate.

Living More of Our Lives

We have many miracles in our lives. Many that we take for granted such as the computer, fax machine or cell phone. We "half read" the operating instructions and proceed to use only a small portion of what each piece of equipment can do. Most times, we are not using the full capacity of these modern miracles. It is not surprising to find that when we get to the matter of our daily lives, we are also only partially aware of the wonderful and miraculous potential in each moment. We sleep walk through a large portion of our lives and go on automatic pilot through the rest. We live in routine, patterned ways and schedule ourselves out of the present and into the future. This is not entirely our fault because once we slip into the unconscious advertising-induced habits that we are enticed to pursue, we are hypnotically driven to distraction and trivial endeavors. We forget to read our owner's manual and we proceed to use only part of our great capacity as human and spiritual beings.

The events of 9/11 took away the certainty of the past and the illusion of a promised future and, in return, gave us an opportunity to live mindfully and meaningfully in the present. On that day, as we were forced into living "in the moment," we became amazing; stretching ourselves to do what must be done without limits or doubts.

When, in a fleeting moment of wakefulness, you glimpse the miraculous potential inside of you, think about asking yourself these questions to kindle a focus on living more of your unique and unduplicated life:

- **How much of my life am I living?**
- **What level am I at right now?**
- **What would be the next level?**

- **How would it feel to be there?**
- **What is my strategy for getting there?**
- **What does being self-expressed mean to me?**
- **What would it be like to be self-expressed?**

Staying awake in our lives is challenging and the very thought of it can often send us into flight, so be aware and examine the things in your life that cause you to go back to sleep: doing too much; neglecting moments of quiet reflection; eating, drinking or indulging too much; being preoccupied with worry, fear, anger and unforgiveness; and failing to be creative.

One way to keep you feeling amazed by yourself is to try this activity: *Think of something amazing about yourself, or something that you have done that is especially impressive or expressive and gently stroke your chin and say, "Mmmmmm, I'm impressed!!!"* I believe that as we adopt this positive habit of noticing ourselves more, we will quickly find ourselves taking up more room in our lives, and we may also find that we have reached the ***next level***.

Rule #2: Look for opportunities to be self-impressed and self-expressed. Keep the memory of those moments to help you through difficult times and to fuel your desire to go to the next fabulous level of your magnificent life.

One Spirit

When we look at our lives, composed of all the things we do; the roles we play; the responsibilities we have, we can see a picture of ourselves in the world. We can measure ourselves against who we started out to be and examine how we've lost or perhaps gained some things along the way. Sometimes it's that we've lost our loved ones, creativity, a sense of fun, health, or possessions. We can look at our key chains and see evidence of the lives we live, as well as what we have determined is important. We can look at the job or relationships we're in and see either what we've settled for, or what we've aspired to. In each instance, we are looking at a partial view of who we are. The mind is a dominant force in the life we live, but when we forget about our body and spirit, we lose in the bargain. When we don't embrace both masculine and feminine principles, we are partially effective.

We often reject opposites and live in one or another extreme. Being one spirit, we embrace the opposites and join all things by connecting to a center; the origin and the destination for all things. In this way, we feel whole and possess strength, clarity and understanding.

Chi, as life force, and qualities of yin (feminine) and yang (masculine) are descriptions of the vital attributes needed to sustain life. Exploring how they appear in our lives is an important step toward unifying spirit and finding our inner power, peace and fulfillment.

What have we forgotten? What do we need to remember? Many think that they have forgotten themselves. Some have forgotten how to be uninhibited and free. Some have sacrificed their feminine nature in order to compete in a male-dominated work arena or profession. With our forgetting, we have lost power and a sense of energy and enthusiasm that we can retrieve beginning with the simple act of remembering, for example, that we are healthy, happy, beautiful, competent, confident, capable, clear thinking, calm and content, strong, safe and secure... that we have boundless energy, unlimited prosperity, peace of mind, joy and bliss.

Taking time to connect with Spirit, and taking it out of the third place, or the corner where it sits waiting for you to remember it, you can reclaim the fullness of who you are and what you are here to express. Invite your Spirit to dance, connect with the Spirits of others on the dance floor and enjoy oneness in a spectacular way.

Rule #3: We are stronger and more able to manage the challenges and enjoy the delights of life when we unify with Spirit and allow it to guide us on the journey.

Straw Into Gold

Our wealth is not merely defined in terms of material possessions or money in the bank. Sources of wealth are abundantly plentiful; however, we must have the eyes to see them. Wealth can be good health, friends, family, time alone, a relaxing environment, a disciplined work attitude, spiritual focus, creativity, talent and skills, love or help when it is needed.

Some sources of wealth are hidden beneath our fears and attitudes of limitation. Often we feel stuck or paralyzed when we try to uncover our wealth. We see wealth as the external trappings of success and good fortune: the luxury car, designer clothes, expensive furnishings or big home.

Sometimes it is the wealth we have traded our precious gifts and creativity for, such as in the tale of Rumpelstiltskin. Sometimes we borrow against our future to have wealth today, or expect that we will be rescued from "poverty" and "scarcity" by a hero only to find that "a hero ain't nothing but a sandwich." This is probably what happened to Vanessa Williams who, early in her career, made some choices that could have ruined her future and career. She, in fact, wasn't ruined because she realized what went wrong and she took charge of redirecting the course of her career. One can imagine the person who coaxed her into doing the infamous photos; he probably can best be thought of as her Rumpelstiltskin; helping her out, then coming later to claim a substantial piece of her future and creativity as payment for the help. By reclaiming her power and true worth, she truly turned straw into gold.

With each act of creativity, we have the potential to turn straw into gold. Rosa Parks took the "straw" of a bewildering racist society and turned it into the "gold" of greater equality. Her creativity produced wealth for a nation. How many times have you taken the "straw" of a few items on the cupboard shelf and turned them into a feast? How often have you heard about someone taking an idea and building a major enterprise?

True and lasting personal wealth begins with our self worth. How do we calculate our worth? What does it mean when we make our personal stock go up? All of these ideas help to forge the beginnings of wealth consciousness that will propel us toward the realization of our loftiest dreams and lasting prosperity.

Rule #4: Stay aware of the true unlimited *currency* of your life that will take you anywhere you choose to go. It's an account that you can always draw on and it automatically replenishes itself. It's always there and you cannot use it up, but you may never tap into it, if you don't realize that it is right there inside you.

Swim With the Swans

One glorious Sunday during the summer, I accompanied my husband to the shore. He went out on a fishing boat and I sunbathed on the beach. There were lots of people fishing off the nearby dock and throwing lines from the shoreline. I was relaxed and serenely grateful for the opportunity to soak up rays and see the waves breaking.

Suddenly, a swan appeared in this scene as if from nowhere and clearly out of context, at least in my mind. I instantly felt an exchange of energy and the overwhelming sense that the swan would meet with peril, but as I continued to watch, I saw it swim right up to the fishermen, around the lines and right into their midst. The grace, beauty and bravery of such an act impressed me. I was not alone. Onlookers marveled with curiosity and awe inspired respect.

In contemplating the theme of self esteem, image and reality, consider the swan. To the viewer, this exquisite creature placidly, calmly glides. This however, is not the entire picture. Just below the surface of the water, the swan's feet paddle furiously; contrasting a vivid image of tranquil confidence, if such a thing can be said to exist for a swan. Maintaining that effortless outer image relies on the activity just below the surface.

Perhaps the lesson is to swim with the swans and keep in mind the whole picture of what we perceive. The celebrities, mentors and role models who we see perform with grace, beauty and confidence are propelled forward by the action and busy movement, similar to the swan's paddling feet. Grace, talent and goodwill are accompanied by discipline and hard work. The secret to self esteem is that image and reality must converge through this formula of combined elements, and each of us has the same underlying purposefulness and innate ability to swim like the swans.

Rule #5: Even what appears to be effortless is not without work. Perhaps it is in large part because of the work that a thing can appear effortless. You can be graceful and frozen in time, without movement and direction, if not for the work that moves you along.

Tending the Vine

Have you seen a grapevine in winter? Have you tasted its sweet fruit or mellow wine? Well, relationships are a lot like the fruit of the vine. We want the tasty fruit, but we don't always have the willingness to tend the vine.

Let's think about what this means in our primary relationships with

Self	**We want good health, but we engage in unhealthy habits.**
Food	**We live to eat, instead of eat to live.**
Money	**We want savings, but at every opportunity we're spending.**
Friends/Family	**We sometimes make our families dependent and then expect them to help us. We define how friends see us. If we complain, discuss problems and act defeated, we won't have friendships that support our future goals, strengths and accomplishments because everything will be seen as a problem.**

We distort these forms of energy and abundance and, as a result, we hurt ourselves with the very things that are supposed to help and nourish us. In other words, if we don't do the work of "tending the vine," the fruit won't be sweet and the wine won't be mellow.

How do we tend the vine? Well, we know that the grapevine looks dry and dead in winter, but there is still life in it. In the grapevine, we are seeing seasons of change just as we see in ourselves and our relationships. All relationships grow out of the primary one we have with ourselves.

Stages of Relationship

SPRING	**We marvel at our newness, potency and resilience.**
SUMMER	**We revel in it.**
FALL	**We see things start to fade.**
WINTER	**We think it is dead because it doesn't look the same.**

Some people interpret this final seasonal change as death, and bury perfectly good relationships. To avoid making this mistake, we must examine our understanding of these changes of state. I see the grapevine as a miracle. Although gray, dry and dead-like, it has life running through its innermost parts. I recall a news report of a 63 year old woman who gave birth. We are constantly altering conventional perception and reality.

The most important relationship you'll ever have is the one that will define all others; namely, the one with yourself. Understand the seasons of change in marriage, friendship, food and money.

Rule #6: To cultivate a first class life you need to be aware of how relationships change over time. Some relationships are prematurely buried because they don't look the same as when they started out.

Wearing Your Self Esteem Like Your Best Hat

We generally speak about self-esteem as the elusive part of a person that once captured can easily, and sometimes without warning, simply slip away into the depths of a deep depression or a pit of despair. We look to retrieve it and often find that the process is one of great difficulty because it easily gets lost among the clutter of our busy lives or the tangled web of our relationships that require constant tending. I often look to find ways to be connected to my self-esteem and suffer greatly in its absence. I counsel others when they find theirs missing or lost, and I stay alert to develop ways to master the technique of maintaining a sense of self-esteem.

I remember attending a workshop on clearing clutter and the presenter opened by saying that you never lose your toothbrush because you always put it in the same place. Perhaps that is the key to sustained self-esteem: Always put it back in the same place. Well, if we don't have a place for it, its elusive nature causes it to move on, so yes we must find and make the place and consistently put it there.

Today, while in my aerobics class, I placed a favorite hat on a hook, along with other articles of clothing and bags. While I exercised, the hat fell from the overloaded hook to the floor. I turned and saw it there, but silently decided to leave it until I could free my attention from the class to pick it up. Well, a woman walked by and came dangerously close to tramping over it, and I suddenly realized that to leave it on the floor would surely lead to someone stepping on it. Valuing my hat, as I do, I quickly picked it up, only to see it fall again. Yet, unlike the first time, I made sure to pick it up and put it on the hook. That is when I learned that self-esteem is like the hat that symbolically represents something that I value about myself, and when I don't take care to keep it placed securely, I risk allowing others to trample over it; misusing or abusing it;

stepping all over it. I like my hat and what it says about me. I know that if I start there, I will be less confused about where I stand when others do things that could potentially hurt me, or shake my belief in myself; so I keep my hat close and my self-esteem closer. Self-esteem is part of our immune system and it sends a powerful message to the world about who we think we are. It tells the people in our lives *"don't tread on me."* It gives us the deep reassurance that we can withstand life's challenges and build rather than lose strength and power. Invest in a good hat and watch your life grow in surprisingly creative and inspiring ways.

Rule #7: When we hold ourselves in high regard others get the idea that they should, also. When we slip and forget where we put our self-esteem; or act carelessly as though it doesn't matter, we send out a signal that we can easily be hurt and mistreated at the drop of a hat.

Be a Tourist

Observing the hectic pace of life, I am often reminded of those fleeting moments when I have strolled the boulevards of Paris; sauntered down Canyon Road in Santa Fe; or sunned myself on the Rivera Maya in Cancun. On those occasions, I have been supremely happy being swept up in the newness, freshness and unpredictability of each experience. I am charged with energy and high spirits and open to the possibilities.

Based on understanding that we are all travelers and new arrivals, I urge you to be the tourist. Approach your day like a tourist on a new adventure in new surroundings. Look at that baby in the carriage and imagine how those tiny dark eyes that dart back and forth are seeing that new day. Imagine that tiny traveler bundled in pink and mother's love as your guide for the new experiences of life.

Rule #8: If you can't step into the same river twice, what makes you think that today is only a carbon copy of yesterday? Be a tourist and put on your traveling shoes while you embark on the greatest adventure of your life: today.

Know that Not Every Closed Door is Locked

In my office, on almost a daily basis, one can see the bathroom door closed and seemingly locked. In a fair number of instances, it is in fact locked because someone has forgotten to unlock it from the inside when exiting. However, there is a percentage of the time when it is closed, but not locked. This peculiar fact has caused me to ponder the larger question related to the ever elusive and desirable life opportunities that can often feel locked behind doors. Well, let me share my personal insight and advice: Try every door because often, although it is closed, it can be opened.

How many times have you wanted to pursue a dream or a goal, only to be convinced that there is no way for you to achieve it, so in your hopelessness, you give up. You want to ask your employer for a raise, but you heard that there are budget cuts and a hiring freeze. This proverbial closed door, keeps you standing outside waiting for someone to open it from the other side. Then after standing there so long, the person who was in there got a raise and promotion and you're waiting and the place is unoccupied.

Rule #9: You don't know how happy, successful, or fulfilled you can be until you try. Take a chance, even if you can't muster the complete confidence and faith that tell you that you can't lose. Knocking at the door ensures that at least one will open.

Don't Make Others Responsible for Your Dreams

If only I had the right breaks; started younger; gotten that advanced degree; didn't have those lousy parents; was taller, thinner, richer, I would make my dream come true. It's not my fault that I can't get out of this slump. I had a setback and now I'm paying for it. My boss is mean and doesn't understand. If only I hit the lottery. He won't let me; she undermines me; they don't like me.

These are the typical reasons that we defer our dreams to life's fortune and default on our responsibility to be the change agents in our own lives. We whine, complain and blame. We do everything, but *wake up* and live the day as though it was a fresh start filled with dream fulfilling possibilities.

What's the best way to get a book published? It's not waiting until you get a response to your query letter, or a literary agent. The best way is to start writing and don't stop until you have a book. What's the best way to overcome a fear of public speaking? Speak. You may say that so and so won't let you talk, or there were no great speakers in your family, or there was that one bad experience. There is no end to reasons, excused and rationalizations for not doing something and they can consume your whole life without ever giving you the satisfaction of simply doing the thing; achieving the goal; embracing the reality of your dream come true.

Rule#10: The dreamer is best suited to creating the conditions to see the dream realized. Others don't have the best sense of what is in your heart and mind and, therefore, if you entrust them with giving you your heart's desire, you will usually be disappointed. Take it on and be the champion of making your dreams reality.

Look for Yourself in Your Enemies

As unlikely as it may seem, we can gain a lot of information and insight just by looking at who we dislike. Simply listen as you recount your tale of woe about that troublesome co-worker; relative or shopkeeper. What did you dislike about them or how they treated you? Was it the fact that they kept you waiting; made you feel "small;" or was it that they ignored you and made you feel "less than." Was it that they didn't acknowledge your title, status or ability? Next, you can ask yourself, "How would you like to see them change?" What would you consider better treatment? Do think they are incapable of any positive change?

Using my own example, I can share how I became enlightened when I searched my soul and found my enemy standing as a mirror reflecting me. I had a colleague who seemed particularly difficult. He would complain that he could not find me when I was usually in my office. He pointed out that my door was always closed, and of course he was correct in that because I find interruptions difficult to manage when I'm trying to complete my work. Our difficulties continued because he would take his concerns to our mutual supervisor. He seemed to want me to be accountable to him in ways that, for me, seemed inappropriate; therefore, I would occasionally be non-responsive to his numerous e-mails. Hoping to clear up our difference, I went to his office on a few occasions, so that we could talk things out and come to some kind of understanding, but met with little success. Finally, perhaps because he tired of the absence of a suitable resolution, the supervisor instituted a monthly staff meeting that had been somewhat delayed because of other demands. At the very first meeting this individual shared his work "style," saying that he expected a prompt response to e-mails as a standard of professionalism. He went on to say that writing things down gave them a higher level of importance that he presumed would alert those who received these communications. He then added that cognitively he had a problem with unannounced, drop-in interruptions. Suddenly, a light went on and I confronted the fact that here sat a person with a set of work values, ethics and standards, not unlike myself. We, simply, operationalized them in different ways. I value the written word, although not copious e-mails. I noted for his and everyone's benefit that I get a very high volume of e-mails and could not possibly answer every one and it's even less likely that I could respond promptly because I am often in meetings or in the field. I confessed that I resort to dropping-in when I think that direct communication would be more effective and I do, in fact keep my door closed as my own method of avoiding interruptions.

So there you have it. We are more alike than different and what is seemingly most interesting is the fact that we both dislike interruptions. From that time, I have respected our differences by honoring our similarities. I believe that what I found true about this interpersonal challenge is true of most of us. I was just granted time and an ability to explore how we are all more alike than different, and if we take the time to understand our enemies, we stumble upon ourselves in the process.

Rule # 11: What we don't like about others, is often what we don't like about ourselves. Rather than challenge ourselves to explore our own inner depths, we often have curious interest in probing the moods, actions or behaviors of others. Use your "enemies" as mirrors of your deeper self.

Be Fabulous

One day while traveling the halls of my workplace on my way to an appointment, I came upon a colleague who greeted me in her characteristically upbeat manner. She asked: "How are you?" Without warning I said, "Fabulous!" As you may imagine, I surprised myself with this response, but having uttered it, I decided to "follow-through" so I said, "I've decided to be *fabulous* all week!" She agreed with my choice; yet, I wasn't sure what it might mean for me to be *fabulous.* After a brief bit of thought, I concluded that to be fabulous would mean that I show up in my life in *fabulous* ways; from the way I looked to the way I walked, talked and thought.

Later in the week, I happened upon another colleague who asked me how I was and I, again, replied "Fabulous!" and explained that that was my chosen state of being for the week. Despite the events of the week, I remained *fabulous,* and I feel that I am better for it because it gave me access to an option that I may have formerly overlooked. It was exciting and energizing to utter that simple reply and I often think of it.

I believe that our intentions can certainly shape our reality and if we focus on the best option we can think of, that can direct us toward a higher standard of living. I'm reminded of another occasion when I decided to seek out a "delicious bran muffin." Having had the experience of tasting a petite, delicious bran muffin at a meeting, I decided that I wanted to re-live the experience. I knew that it would not be easy, but one day while in transit between meetings, I decided to stop at a coffee shop and make my intention known to the clerk at the counter. I said, "I would like to have a *delicious muffin."* Without any gesture of interest or surprise, she moved robotically toward the shelf with the bran muffins and issued mine within the customary bag. When I tasted the muffin, it was clear that she misunderstood the directive and gave me an ordinary, dry and somewhat stale version. Hence, the other part of my lesson was that when I declare an intention for myself, I have a great deal more power to realize it, than if I must depend upon someone else to fulfill my expectations.

Imagine if I relied on my colleagues to deliver a *fabulous* week. There's a great chance, perhaps even a certainty that it would have gotten delayed in the inter-office mail and I would have had to postpone it for another week. Be *fabulous* when you choose to be and know that a fabulous week can make even a mediocre bran muffin taste delicious.

Rule # 12: Be the best you can be and expect the best from yourself, but don't rely on others to fulfill your expectations. Involve them as witnesses rather than the delivery system.

Have a Happy New Day

Many of us can't seem to manage waking up to a new day. Like yesterday's meal, we warm up yesterday and serve it up in twenty year old conversations about the love we lost; the opportunity for advancement that got away; the sickness; or the great wrong that left us wounded and incapable of recovery or forgiveness. It takes awareness and practice to alter the ever present habit of recycling old conversations. The tendency, especially with close friends and family is to use the power of speech to re-hash events, ideas and situations of the past rather than construct sentences based on what is happening at the moment. We struggle to make sense of the past while all the time missing the point of the present.

Some fall short of waking up to a happy new day by interpreting everything in terms of what happened in the past, so today seems strangely familiar and hopelessly inescapable. If we characterize ourselves as unlucky, we remain unlucky until which time as we may choose to wake up to what is happening now. Being so absorbed in past hurts and mistakes, we will unwittingly relive them over and over again.

We can't soar if we are grounded by the heaviness of negative past events. What will happen is that we will appear to take-off, then land just a few feet away, crashing from the weight of our heavy *cargo*. The best way to get "lift-off" is to do what I did when I was the chair of the education department at a small local college. On Monday's I taught a class early in the morning. Because I enjoyed teaching the class, I enjoyed Monday mornings. I noticed that each time I ascended from the depths of the subway station at my stop, I felt like I was being born into a new day; traveling the birth canal of steps while viewing the sky through the opening of the staircase. This always refreshed me and made me feel that I was truly entering a new day. I applied this same idea when working with traumatized women. I used this metaphor to show how one can resist the urge or compulsion to recreate yesterday's pain in each new day. The fact of the matter is, we can wake up and we can make a fresh start. Think about renaming Monday as "New Day" or "Fresh Start." Let your morning commute culminate in your "birthing" ascent into the light of day. Resist the tendency to relive dreadful passages of your past in conversation and recollection; at least until you have greater mastery of having a happy *new* day.

Rule #13: Think of today as your brand new creation, not the hand-me-down of yesterday. Fly toward the bright new possibilities of the day and feel unfettered and free.

Work Is Not a Reason to Live

I have often wondered about the pathways to "burnout." Today, I am confident enough to venture a guess that one pathway is called, "Unfulfilled Expectations." Although we know that work is not a reason to live, we can often substitute work for friends, hobbies, exercise and recreation until work becomes the reason to get up in the morning. We can become so enamored that we indulge it with offerings and gestures of sacrifice such as sleepless nights; extended days; missed medical appointments, and shortened vacations. All of this can happen slowly and without warning. Then the realization dawns on us that life seems without meaning and purpose; or that work seems without meaning and purpose because work has become life. A preoccupation with work as the source and meaning of life conspire to rob the joy from life, and "burnout" becomes the acknowledgement of this fact.

Simple things can begin the process of healing from a state of "burnout." Firstly, we must recognize that work is not life; and it is not our reason for being. If this is a shock, please do not read further.

Perspective tells us that work is one vehicle of expression for our gifts, talents and skills. As such, it can provide us with abundant compensation, recognition and validation; yet, if seen as the only way to receive positive feedback, setbacks; difficulties and failures can feel like deeply personal shame, disappointment or even grief. This goes back to the maxim of putting all your eggs in one basket. One fall, and you've lost everything.

If you find yourself there, take a first step in recovery by giving a bit more to yourself, and then to other aspects of your life. Renew the pleasure of exercising, making contact with friends, taking a mid-day break, seeing a play or taking an art class. Think about what it is that brings you joy, then express it. Seek out the meaningful things in your life even if they are on the shelf and dusty. Don't settle for a limited view of life.

Rule #14: Practice stretching yourself to see over, around and beyond work. If you find that you can't, this may mean that you have allowed it to overtake other meaningful areas of your life. Bring back meaning by seeking a bigger purpose for your life; one that goes beyond the nine to five.

Beware of Secondhand Talk

Several years ago when I first penned observations about a pervasive phenomenon that I referred to as *secondhand talk,* the epidemic was in its beginning stages. Pagers and cell phones the size of wartime walkie talkies were becoming commonplace. Along with this emerging interest in telecommunications, came the disturbingly common practice of secondhand talk. Today, innocent bystanders can be assailed at anytime by the sound of close encounters of the verbal kind in which intimate banter and distracting details can be overheard on subways; at bus stops; in corridors; on park benches and waiting rooms. There is no "high ground" when discussing this issue because we are, by now, all guilty of our share of like offenses. I am merely writing to point out the toxic dangers of over-exposure.

Have you ever left your home cheerful and refreshed, only to arrive at your destination, depressed or full of rage? Sometimes this is the result of contamination from the overheard conversations that can douse you with flames of fury, or a downpour from the broadcast of misdeeds of our fellow human beings. Have you ever heard about the cheating ways a spouse while a small child sits dangerously close by?

If you can't escape, or cover your ears, use this opportunity to practice your own form of mindfulness meditation and focus your attention elsewhere, using all your powers of concentration and restraint. With resolve and intense focus, hear the far off bird songs and church bells that summon you to be at peace in the midst of the *storm.* Your mastery of this practice will be tested daily, and each day you will be able to summon the necessary tranquility to preserve your mood and arrive at your destination without having changed your spirit's manifest.

Rule #15: Look inward toward the depth of a soul at peace and do not let headlines or hysteria rob you of your serenity. If you crave drama, simply learn how to turn it off and on as you would a television or radio.

Put Your Chair Facing the Right Direction

I have a wonderful rocking chair that recalls to me a row of rocking chairs that adorned my grandmother's front porch. I look at this chair; yet, only sit in it occasionally. One morning I realized that I might not sit in it because it faces inward from its position in front of a window. I decided to turn it around and face it toward the window, so that I, too, could face the view of the outdoors in the morning and the evening. In the morning I see the new day being born, and at night I see the moon resting in the sky.

Perhaps this direction is evidence that although we can turn inward for reflection and self-examination, there is a wonderful spectacle that calls to us. Often we miss it because of preoccupation with the busy-ness of daily life. Instead of endlessly walking by the chair that symbolizes joy and peace, I have vowed to enjoy it. And if I seem not to do it often enough, it may be because it is facing the wrong direction. If it faces outward and I need a more inward focus, I will move it until it is in the right place. Likewise, if it faces inward and I am not drawn to sit in it, I will make the necessary adjustment to face it outward. The important thing is to know that the chair is waiting to give me rest and peace in whatever direction I desire.

Rule #16: Honor the four directions and know that life is not linear and joy and peace are not to be passed over. Life's journey is often a matter of being present enough to pause and appreciate the golden moments, but if you're not easily drawn into such awareness, move things around until you find the right direction and view.

Use an Empty Nest for a Needed Rest

The day comes when your young adult leaves for college or takes an out-of-town job; your cat or dog dies; your roommate moves out or puts you out; you and your partner part company or you decide that it's time to clear the clutter that has been a long time "friend" and "companion." Is it time for that *breakdown"* you thought about so often when your youngster came in too late; your dog gave you fleas; your roommate lost the door key, again; your partner interrupted your creative activity with news of their morning commute; you couldn't find your passport on he morning of your overseas flight? Well, they say that in every problem is the solution, so where is yours?

You are wearing black to symbolize your darkened gloom in response to a new aloneness; sense of loss and suddenly you realize that you look good in black. You realize that you don't have to stand in line for the bathroom; your grocery bills show no flea collars; your evening plans are not limited by anything but your imagination; and you can find that telephone number in your computer database in your computer that sits beside your organized book shelves.

Change can help us to grow, pause, and plan new pathways through what can be complicated lives. As we come to understand our lives, we realize that the only thing complicated is our response to the changes in it. Rest in the arc of change and know that it summons a new chapter full of new discoveries and new pleasures.

Rule # 18: Greet aloneness in the same way you would an old friend. Invite it in and enjoy the change it brings.

Relish the Prosperity of Youth

One morning I thought about the *prosperity of youth*—the wealth of opportunity that rests within the young. When we think of youth in these terms, we better understand the meaning of how we "spend" our time. I am forever in conflict with the demands that draw me away from solitary pursuits; moments of rest and fulfilling connections to self and loved ones. I have learned to harmonize with the demands while maintaining a sense of presence in my own life; connected in my life to love and my Source. I have the *prosperity of youth*—it dwells in my spirit, not my body, and I must be careful of how I spend that precious gift.

Right now, standing here I rejoice in the riches of this single moment. A breeze moves through the space cooling my face. I'm standing in comfortable shoes and I feel at peace. Freedom is created by exchanging the bounty of prosperity and getting back change because is less costly than the lack of it.

Rule #19: Cost and value are very different. How we spend our time will have both a cost and a value. Try to get the best deal.

Resist the Urge to Lose at Life

Grief, loss and separation can easily make us feel that we are losing at life—things are taken away such as loved ones, jobs, property, and a fragile sense of safety. We can be seduced into feeling like victims, but we must remember the ocean's ebb and flow; the balance of its movement in and out. Both are of equal value and importance. What would happen if we didn't let the tide go out; didn't let the sun go down; or kept love ones here in the limited reality of flesh and blood existence without a chance for renewal and growth on the spiritual plane?

We sometimes make the premature decision to cut ourselves off due to sorrow and fear of further loss, but the truth is that we are here to experience all that life has to offer; and a large part of experience is letting go of the past, so that the present and future can unfold. We can become afraid to fly and think that we have resolved the issue of safety, but deep down we know that safety means much more than refraining from air travel. It's a lot like a fear we may have about realizing a long-held dream or goal. Because we may have lost out on past opportunities or been rejected by others, it's easy to generalize that it's better not to try.

Life is made up of "bitter" and "sweet" experiences that both teach valuable and important lessons. However, when we feel that we have lost something, we can let that bitterness become a negative thing, or we can focus on how it gives more meaning to what remains in our lives.

Embrace the bitter and sweet parts as parts of the same whole, and understand that to love one is to love both because they complete the picture of what life really is. Prepare to look for ways to see yourself as the fullness and expansiveness of the shore that awaits the departure of the tide and its return. Although it goes away, it returns and brings with it a new array of treasures.

Rule #20: Nothing is ever lost to you as long as you connect and understand its spiritual essence. The myth of separation need not be your reality.

Watch Out For the Ugly Truth

One Saturday while entertaining my grandchildren with their choice of "fast food," I came upon a neighbor of many years who I had not seen for quite some time. Before she noticed me, I saw that she wore a weathered kerchief and equally weathered sneakers. She appeared rather poorly attired from what I remembered of her personal style. As this slight woman of greater years prepared her coffee that accompanied a single small burger, I thought about the thinning hair that was only partially covered by the kerchief.

I would have continued to remain unnoticed by her except that my grandchildren grabbed the seat directly facing her. Although I afforded myself a few more precious moments of anonymity, she finally recognized me and said, "hello," followed in short order with the observation that I had gained weight. This, to me, would usually be cause for a major *meltdown*; however, the years have made me wise and I faced this comment and the person delivering it as the personification of "The Ugly Truth." It came in the form of a balding, elderly woman having a solitary meal. The scene was worthy of a Grimm fairytale.

It wasn't until the following morning, as I prepared for a day at the beach; dressing and looking at my image in the mirror, that I fully appreciated the value of "The Ugly Truth." I surely had gained, and this of course had not escaped my recognition even before her comment, but more importantly, although I had grown in mass, I had also grown in my self-respect. So, in the manner of all learned and esteemed, self-actualized beings, I accepted that no matter what my size, shape, I would love and respect me for all that I am from my fondness for almonds, pecans, and cashews; hot fudge sundaes and fine pastry to my longing for the slender back, slim waist and shapely limbs of my youth, I endure and celebrate that "The Ugly Truth" was born a twin and I share with you that if you are to *take flight* on a journey of unparalleled joy and excitement, you must travel with both "The Ugly Truth" and "The Beautiful Truth" of who you really are.

Rule #21: The opinions of others and your opinion of yourself must never betray your birthright as a magnificent creature of enduring beauty and greatness.

BONUS MATERIAL
SOME ADDITIONAL ROADSIDE ASSISTANCE
Affirmations for the Journey

<u>Be the Change</u>—I am the change. In the words of Gandhi, "Be the change" you want to see in the world. If you want more understanding, be more understanding. If you want to encourage gratitude, express more and be a model of thankfulness. If you want peace and love, be a model of peace and love.

<u>Love</u>—I came from Love and Love is my birthright. This is the only true, everlasting power in the Universe. I am the most powerful when I align with it.

<u>Strength</u>—I have strength. Strength is being gentle with your weaknesses and those of others. It endures and gives substance to your Life because it teaches you humility and wisdom.

<u>Responsibility</u>—I stand upright amid my choices with acceptance and with the courage and determination to grow that comes from loving myself and others.

<u>Acceptance</u>—I start by accepting yourself and then by embracing others.

<u>Truth</u>—I never lie to myself about my magnificence and the magnificence that lies within others.

<u>Gratitude</u>—I am blessed and mindful of it.

<u>Abundance</u>—I breathe, move, swallow, sweat, laugh and repeat; therefore I am healthy and whole and filled with the light of abundance.

<u>Silence</u>—I am silent- In the Silence I understand my divine purpose. I make a gift to myself of least 5 minutes of Silence each day.

WHAT I HAVE LEARNED

I have learned…
Each branch is a tree.

I have learned…
In each moment, we are
Acting on behalf of the Divine.

I have learned…
The more complicated
a truth is professed to be,
the less likely it is to be
true.

I have learned…
There is wisdom in focusing
Without the urgency of
crisis.

I have learned …
That the only thing that you get
When you chase a man (or woman),
Is exhausted.

I have learned …
Patience is the Mother of Change.

I have learned…
It is possible to own your Genius.

I have learned …
Much can be
Gained when you make a Plan and take a
Stand.

I have learned…
Some paint what is in their eye;
Others what is in their heart.

I have learned…
Love is the answer to every question.

I have learned …
Peace is the promise of the
untroubled spirit.

I have learned…
It is better to attack the problem,
Not each other.

SPRING CLEANING

<u>PURPOSE</u>: To re-focus energies in support of personal development, success and well-being.

To rid the mind, body and spirit of accumulated "debris" that obstructs movement and clutters your life; inhibiting growth and harmonious action.

<u>ASSESSMENT</u>: Self Inventory - Complete and review.

<u>ACTION PLAN</u>: FOCUS PLAN PREPARE ACT EVALUATE

Set goals for weeks 1 2 3

WEEK 1

WEEK 2

WEEK 3

Traveling Directions for Women

CLUTTER CLEARING
QUESTIONS

1. DO YOU LOVE IT?
2. IS IT USEFUL? IS IT USED?
3. IS IT IRREPLACEABLE?

"I Caught the Blues From Someone Else"

Song by Bobby Blue Bland

Can you recall a time when you "caught the blues from someone else?"

Describe what happened, how you felt and how you dealt with it.

What happened? (circumstances)

How did it feel? (How did you feel before it happened?)

How did you deal with it? (How did you handle it?)

Self-Actualization Manifesto

Come into the space of Reflection to explore the meaning of your Journey of Life and Begin to Appreciate Every Movement of Change and Experience

Introduction

I learned to drive in the winter during times of ice, snow and rain, so these things do not frighten me when I drive. Likewise, I formulated these thoughts as I went through the snow, rain and ice storms of Life, so I fearlessly introduce them to you as a Bright New Day; Sunrise or Clear Sky to give you confidence as you travel similar roads.

We do not Stop the Rain, we just learn how to Navigate.

First Stop…

Be careful what you commit your Belief to. If I believe that I should have more than I have, I miss the great abundance that already surrounds and engulfs me, and I disrupt the flow of abundance that is already mine.

Proceed…

Stage One
Claim your Gift of Peace

I am at Peace with Who I am
Whose I am

Where I am
What I have
What I do
What I receive
What I give
How I live
When I Change

Understand…

Depression
Cannot heal the World
Cannot heal my sadness about the condition of the World
Or my Life
But it can help me to punish and rob myself

Anger & Unhappiness
Cannot cure a World that is Suffering

Appreciation
If I do something to be Appreciated, I will be Disappointed,
but if I do it to please myself and to Express Love,
Joy or Health I will be Fulfilled and Uplifted

Fear
Is a Night Visitor
Craving the Darkness of my Mood
Poking and Prodding to See if I could be
Consumed as Its Tender Snack

Beauty
Is not Good Looks or Good Luck
It is the Substance of Eternal Truth
And it is Worn Like Grace & Serenity
Draped over Humility
I Celebrate myself through Beauty

Choice
In each Moment I can Choose
Heaven or Hell to Live in
Love is the Wisest Choice

Sacrifice
I Simply place my Love on the Altar and Life is
Renewed And my Soul Reaches toward Eternity

Work & Purpose
My task in each Moment is to be
Loving
Joyful
Healthy

Truth
Love, Silence and Beauty are the Ultimate Truths

Eternity
Is Born in this Moment
Cutting ties to the Past and the Future
While Flowing into the Present Moment
Realizing that I am in the Unified Field of Infinite Possibility

Change
I do not ask the Tiger to be a Lion
But I ask Myself
To Straighten the Crooked Paths Through Change
Leading to the Destination of Love of Self and Others

Living
I can only live one Life at a Time
How many Lives am I trying to Live?
If I try to Live the Life of Another
My Desire to Help, Save or Give them Life
Will actually Rob their Life
Leaving them to Walk the Earth
Without a Spirit of Purpose or Connection
Free them and they will have Life or Rebirth

Greatness
It is a Great Day
I am going to a Great Place
To Do a Great Thing
In a Great Way

Health
I am Whole and Complete

Breath
Connects me to the Divine

Words
Are Vehicles on my Journey to Self-Actualization

But I must First get on Board
They cannot take me there without my Consent
If I use the words, but do not
Understand,
The Journey will be Troubled by Stops and Starts and Break-Downs

Stage Two

<u>Take a Stand</u>…

I Claim
This Present Moment
(My Source of Power and Purpose)
To have and declare Peace & Freedom
I commit myself to being
Loving to Myself
(Loving Who & What I am)

I Claim
Joy as my Birthright and the Currency of my Life
And Live in Joy for its own Sake
Lifted Up and Sustained
As I move through each Moment freely Giving and Receiving Joy

I Claim
Health
The Original Gift
And let it Flow in and through my Cells and my Awareness

I Claim
Wealth

255

Knowing that I am Rich and Fulfilled beyond Measure
I Draw Like Substance to Me at All times

I Claim
Victory
And Arrive Triumphant
In the Land of Light, Peace & Plenty
The Light is Over my Head
And my Open Hands
Give and Receive the
Abundant Blessings that are Mine

I Claim
Fun and Pleasure
As Essential Rest Stops on the Journey of Life
The Quality and Frequency of the Rest
Defines the Best of my Life

I Claim
All that is for my Highest Good
And I Experience my Greatest Rewards
Right Here, Right Now.

Stage Three

Ask Questions...

**What would happen if I traded Faith for
Certainty and Prayer for Meditation?**

What if the Problem is not Out There, but in Here?

What has Supreme Power in my Life?

Make a Plan

1. Stay in the Calm Peace of your Personal Reassurance.
    2. Take Three (3) Deep Breaths when stressed
       or upset, affirming Divine Connection
        3. Get up and get out; keep it moving.

Peace Be the Journey

DREAMS

I claim...
"I have all the time, energy and money
needed to do what is mine to do."
Unlimited Prosperity, Abundance, Health & Joy

Unlimited Business, Personal and Professional Success

Unlimited Insight & Enlightenment

Meaningful, Purposeful, Creative
Action
Thank you.

My Dream List

"Claim your crown...it's your time"

Health	Career/Work
1. 2. 3. 　　　Next...	1. 2. 3. 　　　Next...
1. 2. 3. 　　　Next...	1. 2. 3. 　　　Next...
Personal	Finance

Meditate on the desires of your heart.

Release that which is not for your greatest good.

Today is the day...Right here, right NOW!

I deeply love and approve of myself...

Right here and Right NOW!!!!!

I claim all that is for my greatest good.

<u>Focus</u>　　<u>Plan</u>　　<u>Prepare</u>　　<u>Act</u>　　<u>Evaluate</u>

Theme: "New You"

Renewal and Change are the Gifts We Give Ourselves on the Journey to Our Destiny

Get Ready
"I release and let go, ready to make the most of this present moment."
Unity/<u>Daily Word</u> December 31, 2010

"As I reflect on the events of the past year, I recognize successes and failures, gains and losses. Each event has taught me something and made me wiser. Knowing this, I acknowledge and release the past year in gratitude. In contemplation of the coming year, whether I am excited or apprehensive, I know the spirit of God will empower me to meet every situation with confidence and strength. With this in mind, I release any concerns I may have about the future. Today I am ready to stand tall in this present moment. I appreciate the now, perfectly balanced between the past and the promise of the future. This is the moment of power and action. I am ready!"
"He has made everything suitable for its time." Ecclesiastes 3:11

Choices
By Sue Bryan
Unity Daily Word January 2011

"I listen.

I know what I know.

If it doesn't feed me,

I can choose differently.

If it pains me,

I can walk away.

If it fill my heart with joy, I can spend more time with it.

It is my life.

The choices are mine."

Set Your Agenda for the New Year

I.   Establish your goals.

II.   Determine what will be the evidence
of success in meeting them.

III.   Be on your side.

IV.   Don't waste time in living the lives of others or in
lengthy stays in the past or the future. Use your time well.

V.   Get lighter in mind, body and spirit, so
the journey can be well managed.

VI.   Drink water upon waking.

VII.   Eat five fruits and vegetables during
your day as often as you can.

VIII.   Try interval training with your
walking routine (slow/fast/slow)

IX.   Breathe In and Out: in/safety; out/worry; in/security/
out/fear; in/support; out/burdens; in simplicity; out/
overdoing; in/silence; out/chatter; in serenity; out/confusion

X.   Use "I" statements more often than "she, he, we and they"

XI.   Remember as in "Shakespeare in Love" they kept saying
it would all turn out alright and when asked "how" the
reply was always "I don't know, it's a mystery..." Enjoy the
MYSTERY and become the best NEW YOU you can imagine!

XII.   <u>Get Started</u>

1.   Open your last year's letter to yourself.

2.   Write your New Year's letter in the 1st 7 days of the New Year.

3.   Put the letter in an envelope in a safe
place to be read next year.

4.   Keep your goals in plain sight.

5.   Invest in your health.

6. "Put First things First"—Stephen Covey
(ie. Health, family, friends, etc).
7. Use everything you have (integrity, honesty,
creativity, clothes, hours in the day.

Goals:

Measures of Success:

Supporters:

Welcome to the Year of Positive Transformation
Theme: "Look Up"
"It is better to be prepared for an opportunity and not
have one than to have one and not be prepared."
Whitney M. Young, Jr.

By "looking up" we see opportunity coming
and we can seize the moment to be alive.
Sharon M. Cadiz

Everyday is Christmas/Chanukah, Kwanza/Diwali/New Year's Day, Harvest Time.
Enjoy Peace on Earth; Sacred Songs; Creative Gifts and put on the Lights.

Everyday is someone's birthday. Celebrate it and light the candles.

Look up instead of burying your head in a newspaper filled with bad news and despair.

Instead of looking down at the cracks in the sidewalk, look up and see the sun bursting onto the horizon.

Instead of looking down at your neighbor, friend or loved one for an error or failing, look up and see them as a child of the Divine, just like you.

Instead of looking down at your watch to tell the time, look up to the heavens and read the journey of the sun across the sky.

Instead of living in a darkness of a moonless night sky, look up and marvel at the greater visibility of the stars.

Instead of contemplating the end of your Life, look up and remember that the Spirit's journey is unending.

Instead of thinking about the end of the world, look up and know that you are the Phoenix rising out of the ashes to claim a new beginning founded on Love.

Look up and Go Within in these Winter Months:
Reflect

*"There is a privacy about it which no other season gives you....
In spring, summer and fall people sort of have an open season on each other;
Only in the winter, in the country, can you have longer, quiet stretches when you can savor belonging to yourself."* Ruth Stout

"Let us love winter, for it is the spring of genius." Pietro Aretino

"Consult not your fears but your hopes and your dreams. Think not about your frustrations, but about your unfulfilled potential. Concern yourself not with what you tried and failed in, but with what it is still possible for you to do." Pope John XXIII

Quotations for the Change Journey

From **This Year I Will… by M.J. Ryan**

"Time is a created thing. To say "I don't have time" is to say, "I don't want to." Lao Tzu

"I hope to remind people like me that we have the strength and ability to do anything we want. Losing weight is a choice the same as continuing to exist in this terrible condition is a choice. I have decided to live! It really is a simple decision when you think about it." Steve Vaught

"Your compulsive, obsessive, and addictive behaviors each show you frightened parts of your personality…They are your avenues to—growth." Gary Zukav

From **It's Not About the Money by Brent Kessell**

It is only when you understand what your unconscious mind believes about your financial lot in life, what it believes is going to make you happy or safe, that you have a chance to change the tale you're constantly playing in your head."

"Your Core Story represents the deepest-held feelings and beliefs we have about money, what we are unconsciously telling ourselves we are like, what we can and can't have and what we must and must not do… This idea is explained in slightly different terms by **Thich Nhat Hanh**. This prominent Vietnamese Zen Buddhist says it's as if each of us had a basement in our mind in which we stored hundreds of movies about how things should change to make us happy, about who is to blame for our pain, about what's wrong with our life. The astounding thing is that the more we replay the movie, the more the events in our life begin to resemble the plot of that movie".

From **Wayne Dyer:**
One of the most common kinds of habituated self-debilitating ideas concerns money. *I don't have enough money* is a misaligned thought because money is in inexhaustible supply of the world. There is so much of it, in fact, that it would be impossible to create a calculator large enough to even count it.

From **Living a Charmed Life** by Victoria Moran
"Slow down…When we take our time, we have more of it."
"The only time your inner epicure will get out of hand and start pillaging chocolate shops and picking up traveling salesmen is when you deny her until she can't take it anymore."
"Your inner chaperone helps you live successfully by showing you where "peak experience" stops and "downhill from here" begins."

From **Loving What Is** by Byron Katie
"Suffering is optional…"

"The left brain weaves its story in order to convince itself and you that it is in full control…What is so adaptive about having what amounts to a spin doctor in the left brain? The interpreter is really trying to keep our personal story together. To do that, we have to learn to lie to ourselves… We tend to believe our own press"

The Work is an ongoing and deepening process of self realization not a quick fix."

<u>Self Care Plan</u>

I. What are you already doing?

II. What would you consider?

III. What would you like to try?

IV. When would you start?

V. When would you work it into your schedule?

VI. What do you think would be the benefits to you?

Activities

MIND

BODY

SPIRIT

Walk, Don't Run

Our lives tend to be compartmentalized into areas of functioning or roles that serve to give us purpose and meaning. Sometimes we experience hardships, setbacks or stress in certain areas or compartments of our lives. Bringing awareness to this can help to produce healing and recovery.

Another way to promote healing is to "take stock" of what is in our *closets*. Our inner lives are a lot like closets. We store up many things from the past and pile up things we believe we need until we can't determine why we thought they were important or necessary in the first place. We re-buy the very things that were long ago lost and unused in our *closets*, so we need to make a list and go shopping in our closets for all the things we may foolishly think we are without such as beauty, wealth, energy, health, peace and more.

Finding a metaphor for your setback or stress can help you to find your way back to the path. Are you in heavy traffic; a storm; lost at sea; on thin ice, on egg shells; in a drought, wilderness, desert; on a mountain or crowded street? Are you speeding past your joy? Are you stuck in transitions that are only supposed to be temporary, such as a mid-life crisis, career change, grief, loss or separation? Knowing how these things make you feel and what they mean can help you understand how you got there and how to free yourself.

Other dimensions that contribute to a lack of ease are the *speed and transitions* of our lives. As we undergo this inner exploration, we find that we can exercise the option to slow down, change our minds, re-name/re-frame, consider alternatives, unlimit ourselves, coach ourselves with positive messages and safeguard our passage by being mindful of such things as: pace, safe crossings, comforting words, complementary therapies, action plans, celebrations of milestones, clarifying moments.

Being a moving target, at times, means that when sadness or despair look for you in your old haunts where you curl up in self doubt or fear, they find you not there. Thinking of yourself as *precious* and *complete* will help you to instantly feel better. Holding that thought may take a little discipline and practice, but ultimately, it can give you greater immunity to the stresses of life.

When bad times come knocking the next time, you will have a memory of your victories that brought you through the last time. If you were running, you would not have noticed anything, so remember: Walk, Don't Run!!!

Learn to Pause

*"Harmony is the inner cadence of contentment we feel when the melody of life is in tune. When somehow we're able to strike the right chord—to balance the expectations of our families and our responsibilities in the world on the one hand with our inner needs for spiritual growth and personal expression on the other…Usually, when the distractions of daily life deplete our energy, the first thing we eliminate is the thing we need most; quiet, reflective time. Time to dream, time to think, time to contemplate what's working and what's not, so that we can make changes for the better…*Learn to Pause.*"*
By Sarah Ban Breathnach/from <u>Simple Abundance</u>

The act of pausing is a very valuable addition to a person's life because it allows the needed time to gather ones thoughts and perhaps contemplate next steps or a recent accomplishment. I rank "pausing" right up there with money. It's an important form of currency that I recommend you keep in your change purse. Sometimes it will fall out just when you need it to remind you to stop and take a breather before moving on. You will see it when you go into your purse to buy another useless object and it might remind you that you really don't need that thing at all. To help you integrate this helpful practice, I am including some copies of the word "PAUSE" for you to copy and cut out, if you like. I keep mine, as I mentioned, in my change purse. If you do use them, I believe you will start to gain a significant appreciation for the power and benefit that can be derived from taking a "time out."

Pause   *Pause*

Pause   *Pause*

The Road Not Taken
By Robert Frost
(1874-1963)

Two roads diverged in a yellow wood,
And sorry I could not travel both
And be one traveler, long I stood
And looked down one as far as I could
To where it bent in the undergrowth;
Then took the other, as just as fair,
And having perhaps the better claim,
Because it was grassy there
Had worn them really about the same,
And both that morning equally lay
In leaves no step had trodden black.
Oh, I kept the first for another day!
Yet knowing how way leads on to way,
I doubted if I should ever come back.
I shall be telling this with a sigh
Somewhere ages and ages hence;
Two roads converged in a wood, and I—
I took the one less traveled by,
And that has made all the difference.

RESOURCES

www.hayhouse.com

www.BeWildWoman.com

www.classicalstretch.com

www.womenshealth.gov

www.girlshealth.gov

www.sealedwithlove.com

www.iamrecovery.com

www.namastereiki.com

www.herbalintervention.com

www.lavidafemme.com

www.LalitasYoga.com

www.sacredvibes.com

www.alessandrabelloni.com

www.relaisvillalina.com

www.ackproduction.com

www.powerofonecenter.com

www.mayabreuer.com

www.tenthousandvillages.com

www.gaiam.com

www.teaoflife.com

www.seredipitea.com

www.soaringproject.com

COPYRIGHT
ACKNOWLEDGEMENTS

<u>The Art of Peace: Teachings of the Founder of Aikido</u>, Morihei
  Ueshiba translated by John Steven, 1992. Shambhala.

<u>The Game of Life and How To Play It</u>, Florence Scovel Shinn

<u>Joy</u>, compiled by Evelyn Loeb. 1991. Peter Pauper Press, Inc.

<u>Life Lessons for Women</u> by Cindy Francis. 1992. Newport House,
  Inc.

<u>Meditation: Techniques to Try</u> by Chimnoy, S. Jharna-Kala Card
  Co. Jamaica, NY.

<u>Me: Five Years From Now: the Life-Planning Book You Write
  Yourself,</u> 1990. The Stonesong Press, Inc./A time Warner
  Company

<u>Poems of Flowers</u> edited by Gaily Harvey, 1991. Avenel Books/
  Outlet Bood Company, Inc.

<u>Quiet Places with Mary: 37 Guided Imagery Meditations</u> by
  Powers I, 1991. Twenty Third Publications, CT.

<u>Tao Te Ching</u> translated by Stephen Mitchell, 1988. Harper
  Perennial/Harper Collins Publishers.

<u>Time for Myself: Quiet Thoughts for Bust Women</u> by Janet
  M. Congo, Julie L. Mask, and Jan E. Meier, 1993. Thomas
  Nelson Publishers: A Janet Thom Book.

READING LIST

Suggested Reading

Andrews, T. <u>How to Heal with Color</u>

Borysenko, J. <u>Minding the Body, Mending the Mind</u>

Boyd, J.A. <u>In the Company of My Sisters: Black Women and self Esteem</u>

Blanke, G. <u>In My Wildest Dreams: Living the Life You Long For</u>

Chopra, D. <u>Perfect health: the Complete Mind/Body Guide</u>

Day, L. <u>The Healing Circle: An Experience in Recreating Your Life and Living Your Dreams</u>

DeAngelis, B. <u>Real Moments: Discover the True Secret for True Happiness</u>

Dyer, W. <u>The Power of Intention</u>

Estes, C. P. <u>Women Who Run With the Wolves</u>

Foley, D., E. Nechas et al. <u>Women's encyclopedia of health and Emotional Healing</u>

Freudenberger, H., G. North <u>Women's Burnout: How to Spot It/ How to Reverse and How to Prevent It</u>

Gandy-Jackson, D <u>Sacred Pampering Principles: An African-American Woman's Guide to Self-Care and Inner Renewal</u>

Hay, L. <u>Self Healing: Creating Your Health</u>

Hay, L. <u>I Love My Body</u>

Hay, L. <u>You Can Heal Your Life</u>

Hesse, H. <u>Siddhartha</u>

Hudson, C.M. <u>The Complete Book of Massage</u>

Johnson, S. <u>One Minute for Myself</u>

Katie, B. Loving What Is

Katie, B. Who Would You Be Without Your Story

Kornfield, J. Buddha's Little Instruction Book

Lakein, A. How to Get control of Your Time and Life

Louden, J. The Woman's Retreat Book: A guide to Restoring, Rediscovering and Reawakening Your True Self

MacLaine, S. Going Within: A Guide for Inner Transformation

Moran, V. Lit From Within

Moran, V. Creating a Charmed Life

Patent, A. You Can Have It All

Peale, V. Inspiring Messages for Daily Living

Prudden, S. Change Your Mind, Change Your Body

Rubin, G. The Happiness Project

Ruiz, D.M. The Four Agreements

Sherwood, K. The Art of Spiritual Healing

Sherwood, K. Chakra Therapy for Personal Growth and Healing\

Siegel, B. Peace, Love and Healing

Tolle, E. The Power of Now

Williamson, M. The Gift of Change: Spiritual Guidance for Living Your Best Life

NOTES TO MYSELF